NOTES ON CHOSEN ENGLISH TEXTS

General Editor: NORMAN T. CARRINGTON, M.A.

SHAKESPEARE
ROMEO AND JULIET

BY
NORMAN T. CARRINGTON, M.A.

JAMES BRODIE LTD.
15 QUEEN SQUARE, BATH, SOMERSET, ENGLAND

CONTENTS

ROMEO AND JULIET

The Author

Surprisingly little is known of the life of our greatest dramatist, and the little we know is derived mainly from brief references to his name in legal and other formal documents. He was born in Stratford-on-Avon, and, although the exact date of his birth is unknown, there is a record that he was christened William on 26th April, 1564, the third child of John Shakespeare, a man variously described as glover, wool-dealer, farmer and butcher. Until about the year 1578, when his business seems to have begun to decline, John Shakespeare was a notable figure in Stratford, and it is probable that William was educated at Stratford Grammar School, where he may have learned the "small Latin and less Greek" for which Jonson gave him credit. However this may be, the next thing we know that can be accepted as reliable is that on 27th November, 1582, he took out a licence for marriage with a certain Anne Whateley. It was annulled next day, however, upon information laid by the sponsors of another Anne (Anne Hathaway), who claimed a better right for her to be married to William, since she was with child by him. At the age of eighteen, therefore, he married Anne Hathaway, a woman eight years older than himself, and by 1585 three children had been born of the marriage. In this year he is thought to have left Stratford for London. Tradition has it that his departure was owing to trouble over deer-stealing in the grounds of Sir Thomas Lucy, but in the light of modern research it would appear that he left with a band of strolling players, the Queen's Players, who visited Stratford in 1585. His unwilling marriage to Anne Hathaway may have had something to do with his decision to leave his native town.

Whether his wife and children ever lived with him in London is not known for certain, but it is very unlikely, nor is it known what he himself did there before 1592. From a pamphlet published in that year by Robert Greene, a lesser playwright, however, we have news of him as actor and playwright. Plague caused the theatres to be closed

in 1593, and on their re-opening in the following year
we know that Shakespeare was a member of the Lord
Chamberlain's Company (known, after the accession of
James I, as the King's Men), and it is probable that he
stayed with this company for the remainder of his career,
writing plays for it and acting with it in various theatres.
His connection with the company must have brought him
considerable financial reward, for we know that in 1596 his
father, presumably aided by his successful son, applied to
the College of Heralds for the right to assume a family coat
of arms, and in the following year the playwright purchased
(for £60!) New Place, one of the largest houses in Stratford.
Although the house is no longer there, the foundations
can be seen and the garden is open to the public. As
his fortunes prospered, Shakespeare bought shares in two
theatres, the Globe, built in 1599, and the Blackfriars,
built in 1609, so that, in addition to his pay as actor and
writer, he would receive his share of the profits on these
investments.

Thus in 1611, when still under fifty years of age, Shakespeare retired to his native town, a fairly wealthy man,
though he seems to have kept up a connection with London,
as he was concerned in a legal dispute over the purchase
of a house in Blackfriars in 1615. He died in Stratford-òn-
Avon, survived by his wife and two daughters, on 23rd
April, 1616, and was buried in the Parish Church, where
thousands of people from all over the world visit his grave
every year.

As an actor Shakespeare does not seem to have been
eminent, but even in his own day his fame as a dramatist
was very great. Thus Meres in 1598 described him as "the
most excellent in both kinds" (*i.e.* in comedy and in
tragedy) and even Ben Jonson, whose dramatic work was
in a very different vein from that of Shakespeare, remarks
in his *Discoveries*, "I lov'd the man and do honour his
memory (on this side idolatry) as much as any".

Shakespeare probably began his work as a dramatist by
collaborating with others and patching up old plays which
his company wished to revive. His first completely original
play is believed to be *Love's Labour's Lost* (1591?), though
the date of each play is itself a problem, since the dates
are not given in the First Folio (the first collected edition

of his plays, 1623). His non-dramatic works consist of two narrative poems, *Venus and Adonis* (1593) and *The Rape of Lucrece* (1594), and the one hundred and fifty-four sonnets published in 1609—without Shakespeare's permission it is thought. The first one hundred and twenty-six of the sonnets are addressed to a young man, the poet's friend and patron; the remainder to a "dark lady", and the identity of neither of these two is established, though it is tempting to believe that the "dark lady" was Anne Whateley; nor is it decided how far, if at all, the series may be considered autobiographical. Most of Shakespeare's plays were written for performance in the public playhouses, and they were conveniently classified in the First Folio in three groups—comedies, histories and tragedies. But when considered chronologically they seem to fall naturally into four periods, thus admirably described by Professor Dowden.

> First, from about 1590 to 1595-96, years of dramatic appren-
> ticeship and experiment; secondly, from about 1595-96 to about
> 1600-01, the period of the English historical plays and the
> mirthful and joyous comedies; thirdly, from 1601 to about
> 1608, the period of grave and bitter comedies and of the great
> tragedies; last, from about 1608 to 1611 or 1613, the period of
> the romantic plays, which are at once grave and glad, serene
> and beautiful.*

Professor Dowden names these periods respectively "In the workshop", "In the world", "Out of the depths", "On the heights". *Romeo and Juliet* belongs to the first period. It was Shakespeare's first masterpiece. Its exact date cannot be determined, but all the evidence points to some time between 1592 and 1595 or early 1596. It is, indeed, very likely that the play was in Shakespeare's mind for a long time, and was first written in 1592 and subsequently revised and enlarged.

* *Shakspere Primer*, p. 47, published by Messrs. Macmillan and Co. Ltd., whose permission for its reproduction is hereby thankfully acknowledged.

Source of Plot

Shakespeare "lifted" the plot from Arthur Brooke's long poem *The Tragicall Hystory of Romeus and Juliet* (1562), an Italian story which Brooke found in a French translation by Boisteau. It is probable that Shakespeare also read a prose version of Boisteau's story by William Painter (*The goodly History of the true and constant love betweene Romeo and Julietta*) in the second volume of his *Palace of Pleasure* (1567). There was, too, a play on the story (since lost) which Brooke mentions in his Preface *To the Reader* ("the same argument lately set forth on stage") and Shakespeare, an up and coming young dramatist, may have seen it—indeed, if he had done, this would not be the only occasion on which he took his inspiration from the contemporary theatre. This is only guess-work, however, and it has to be remembered that for Shakespeare to be familiar with it the play to which Brooke refers must have kept the stage for at least twenty years.

Shakespeare was not an original playwright: time and time again he built great works of art out of the well-known stories of his day, which only seem "Shakespearean" to us because we do not know his minor contemporaries.

Treatment of Plot

What is more important is Shakespeare's treatment of the plot. As usual he took somebody else's story and gave it new life and new beauty. But since he follows Brooke's poem very closely his divergences therefrom have all the more significance. They were evidently deliberate. For the sake of convenience his chief alterations are put under separate headings.

Compression of Time

Shakespeare compresses the nine months' action of Brooke's poem into less than five days, in the interests of swiftness, power and unity of action.

The movement of the play is clearly marked, according to the following time-table.

Sunday. The play opens with a street brawl at nine o'clock in the morning. Romeo and Juliet first meet at a party the same night. After the party Romeo gets into Capulet's garden and from the ground talks to Juliet at her window.

Monday. They are married in the afternoon. Thereafter Romeo kills Tybalt and is banished, but he defies the law to spend the night with Juliet. Late that night old Capulet arranges Juliet's marriage with Paris for Thursday morning.

Tuesday. As dawn breaks Romeo leaves Juliet. He has no sooner gone than Juliet is told by her parents that she is to marry Paris, and in despair she goes to Friar Laurence's cell.

Late that night the wedding is advanced to take place next morning.

Before she goes to sleep Juliet takes the Friar's draught.

Wednesday. At early dawn Juliet is discovered "dead", and is taken to the family tomb later in the day.

Thursday. Romeo hears of Juliet's death and buys poison.

Friday. During the very early morning, while it is still dark, Romeo comes to the tomb, and the rest of the play takes place before full dawn.

The student will probably get a surprise when he sees this time-table set out, for although swift when its time is analysed the play is not so swift in its general impression. Juliet tells Romeo that their love is "too rash, too unadvised, too sudden" and

> This bud of love, by summer's ripening breath,
> May prove a beauteous flower when next we meet.

When they next meet, therefore, the audience has the impression that there has been a delay, but the delay, in fact, is only a matter of hours. The Nurse tells Romeo that she angers Juliet *"sometimes"* and tells her "that Paris is the properer man"; she speaks as if she has known Romeo a long time, and, according to Juliet, has praised him "above compare so *many thousand* times", yet, in fact, she has known him for only a couple of days. Thus an impression is given of a longer acquaintance, which seems more normal and credible and assists in that "willing suspension of disbelief" which is necessary to enjoy any fiction. It seems as if Romeo has been longer banished than a day when he has had time to take such note of shops and shopkeepers round about. Above all, the growth of the character of Juliet from girl to woman has the strongest effect in lengthening the time-sense. And at the end, after being crossed in love for four days, Romeo talks of "this world-wearied flesh".

Development of Characters

It would be a mistake to think that the borrowing of the outline of the story in any way detracts from Shakespeare's genius. The plot is the least important part of a play. Shakespeare's great artistic power is in characterisation, and through it a story which in inferior hands would be crude and improbable becomes real and lifelike. Invention is not the great artistic quality, but insight—the conception the artist has of life as a whole. A story with a "realistic" plot has no life if the characters are wooden, but a crude plot becomes alive when living people inform it. Artistic creation bears the same relation to plot as architecture to bricks and mortar. Shakespeare was often very careless in his plots; it is in his *use* of the plot that he shows his imagination.

The plot of *Romeo and Juliet* is no exception. It is very thin at its central point, and the amount of coincidence is incredible. Apart from the use of a drug producing a death that is not death, it is unnatural that when Juliet is found "dead" in bed none of the household should suspect suicide or foul play (especially in view of her known reluctance to marry Paris), that no one should want to find out the cause of her death, and that no one should see the empty vial and the dagger by her side. (Shakespeare appears to have forgotten these.) But things like this have little weight. *Romeo and Juliet* is one of the world's greatest plays because Romeo and Juliet are what Shakespeare has made them.

Two important people, developed by Shakespeare from mere names into characters of his own, are Mercutio and the Nurse. They are both outside the main line of progress of the play, but have a bustling vitality in their own right.

They are introduced for contrast—Mercutio with Romeo, and the Nurse with Juliet—and also for wit and comic relief.

Tybalt is another character developed by Shakespeare, and again the dramatic reason is the same, for contrast—with Romeo.

The events of Shakespeare's plays depend on the characters of the people in them, not on an arbitrary fate: it was the natures of Mercutio and Tybalt which caused Romeo's banishment.

Shakespeare takes two years off Juliet's age. According to Brooke, "Scarce saw she yet full sixteen years". It may seem to many that an older girl would have been more credible. Presumably the alteration was to throw into relief her development from an obedient girl to a self-assured heroine—the younger she is to begin with the more noticeable is the fullness of her character at the end. It should be remembered also that on Shakespeare's stage the part would be acted by a boy of about this age (see p. 47).

Poetry and Imagery

The student has only to go to a reference library and read a few of Brooke's long, heavy-footed, unvaried rhyming lines to see how Shakespeare's poetry and imagery owe *nothing* to him. The beauty of Shakespeare's language is a continual joy to every generation. Many passages in the play are worth committing to memory, and some of the most beautiful are among those listed on page 122. More will be said of Shakespeare's style in the appropriate section on pages 40-44.

Construction

There is, in *Romeo and Juliet*, no sub-plot. The construction is simple and straightforward, without any side-issues from the main track. After Act I our whole attention is focused on the love of Romeo and Juliet. Rosaline influences Romeo in Act I but, by Shakespeare's true dramatic instinct in concentrating attention on Juliet, we are made aware of it only by hearsay—she never appears.

The way Shakespeare speeds up the action has already

been noticed in detail (pp. 8-9)—everything is finished in under five days. This, too, gives dramatic concentration. It emphasises the suddenness of the love of Romeo and Juliet, love at first sight, aroused in a moment and soon to be opposed. But notwithstanding this, Act I leans forward and would do with clipping back; the talk about Rosaline could with advantage be cut down. The knowledge that Romeo had been in love with someone else is enough without its amplification to this extent. All that is necessary is that the audience should realise the power of their mutual love to reverse the previous trend of their life, when Romeo was in love with someone else and Juliet unaffected by love. The play proper does not begin until Act I, Scene v, and Scenes ii, iii and iv (at this length) reduce the dramatic concentration and are slow by comparison with the rest.

Some of the speeches in the play are too long for what they accomplish dramatically, for example, those of the Friar as a whole, and, indeed, one or two of the longer speeches of Romeo and Juliet, judged dramatically, that is, not poetically. *Romeo and Juliet* is a lyric play, with much poetry that advances the plot but little—"How silver-sweet sound lovers' tongues by night".

The climax, the marriage of hero and heroine, comes early in the play. Act III, Sc. i is the turning point, and thereafter the fortunes of Romeo and Juliet quickly go downhill until the catastrophe in the last scene. Mercutio's witty tongue was getting him more attention than Romeo's, so he is removed out of the way, and at the same time his death provides a reason for Romeo to take Tybalt's life and so run himself into banishment. The two duels are Shakespeare's means of bringing these events about. At the end Paris is brought into the general cataclysm by another duel.

Elizabethan (like modern) audiences enjoyed blood and battle stuff, and Shakespeare tried to satisfy them. Like any other dramatist he did his best to get a full house, and he wanted people to go and tell their friends that *Romeo and Juliet* was an exciting play that they must not miss. The play is constructed in a way to satisfy them; there is conflict all the way through, from duel and street brawl in the first scene, to duel, murder and suicide in the last, again, so we are told, with a disordered populace shrieking in the streets. It was not Shakespeare's intention that these scenes should be underplayed.

In any play there is a clash of personalities or of wills. This it is that makes the play. Notice the clash in this play between age and youth, between Capulets and Montagues in general, which itself contrasts with the passionate love of two of the young members of these houses, between the Prince and these rebellious families, and, in particular, between Rosaline and Juliet (though not strongly marked), between Romeo's affected love for Rosaline and his real love for Juliet, between the love of Paris and of Romeo for Juliet, between Mercutio and Tybalt, Romeo and Tybalt, Juliet and her parents (and later her nurse), and between Romeo and his friends owing to his absorption in love, especially between Mercutio's wit and Romeo's. Contrast is a fundamental principle in Shakespearean drama, and the student should notice how the play is constructed to bring out such contrasts.

There is very little comic relief to throw up the tragedy in *Romeo and Juliet*, in this respect so unlike Shakespeare's later tragedies. The garrulous chatter of the Nurse and the talk of the musicians after they have found that they are not wanted are the only examples in the play of more than a line or two. Mercutio's witty repartee is on a higher plane than the Nurse's common gossip. The musicians' chatter comes in between the discovery of Juliet dead (to all outward appearances) and Romeo's hearing of her death, both tragic scenes. Romeo's momentary elation just before the news comes has the same effect, to throw the tragedy of her death into more stark relief, so that it stands out more boldly from its surroundings.

Much in the play depends on coincidence (see p. 10), but particularly in the last two scenes: the Friar's letter never reached Romeo, Paris happens to come to the tomb at the same time as Romeo, Romeo kills himself only a few moments before Juliet awakes, and the Friar on such a matter of life and death is late. (One might also include the death of Montague's wife, added to complete the overwhelming sense of destruction.) The greater element of chance in *Romeo and Juliet* makes the events seem less related to the characters of the principals than in Shakespeare's later plays. Their fate is not so much caused by their own actions and characters.

As usual in Shakespeare's plays there is little attention to detail. The effect of the Friar's potion was to wear off after "two and forty hours" (a most exact time—not "about two days"), yet Juliet is asleep after fifty hours (see p. 9), and the Friar, who *expected* her to awake after forty-two hours and might well have made sure by being there before, fails to arrive until some eight or nine hours later than this.

But students should remember that details like this, which are noticed when one *reads* the play, comparing passage with passage, would go unnoticed by an audience in the theatre. Shakespeare constructed his plays without regard for gritty little details (see pp. 16-17), but with much regard for their general pattern.

The student should consider whether the reconciliation scene at the end improves the play or whether it is a superfluous anti-climax (see also p. 16). Has the loss of the lovers made too great an impression for anyone to bother about a reconciliation between their elders?

It is but seldom that Shakespeare uses a Prologue (or Chorus). The Prologue is a device from ancient Greek drama, where the Chorus commented on the events in a detached sort of way. In *Henry V* Shakespeare uses a Chorus to tell of what he cannot represent to the eye, rather than cripple the progress of the action by long (undramatic) descriptions in the mouths of his characters. Shakespeare's usual method is to set the scene for the audience in the conversation of minor characters before the principals enter, which makes the play seem more real. He follows this method here, too, and the Prologues to Acts I and II are not really necessary. Some have therefore wondered if they are by Shakespeare, especially the second Prologue, whose verse is much less distinguished, but to the Editor it seems a dangerous practice to say that inferior passages in the plays must be from some other hand than Shakespeare's, without corroborative evidence from another source.

Atmosphere and Theme

The theme of *Romeo and Juliet* is a consuming love. It is a story of hatred overcome by that love, old hate versus young love, taking no thought for the past or the future. And this love ends in "love-devouring death".

The atmosphere is one of passion and swiftness, full-blooded passion and rash swiftness. Consuming love calls for haste—"Gallop apace, you fiery-footed steeds"—and cannot brook delay. "From nine till twelve is three long hours." The whole play is in a hurry—speed into marriage, speed into banishment, speed back to Juliet, speed in another quarter to get Juliet married to Paris, speed to kill whoever steps in the way and speed to commit suicide when life suddenly seems not worth living. Romeo's haste makes him happy in his marriage, and immediately thereafter unhappy in his banishment, for had he not so precipitately gone for Tybalt's blood he would never have been banished. *Romeo and Juliet* is a play of whirlwind and storms, full of angry feud, tremendous passion and sudden death. Like Othello, Romeo loves "not wisely, but too well".

Even when things are going well there is a sense of impending tragedy in the air, a grim foreboding that makes happy folk mistrust their happiness. The first Prologue speaks of "A pair of star-cross'd lovers" before the play proper starts. The first scene of the play shows how affairs are like powder waiting for a match, and there are those about only too glad to bring one. There is a nameless dread before Romeo has ever set eyes on Juliet.

> My mind misgives
> Some consequence yet hanging in the stars
> Shall bitterly begin his fearful date
> With this night's revels and expire the term
> Of a despised life closed in my breast
> By some vile forfeit of untimely death.

After they have met, both have a presentiment that their love shall end in disaster. Romeo comes to marry Juliet with a challenge to fate on his lips—"Then love-devouring death do what he dare". And Juliet, as she looks on Romeo (alive) for the last time, admits

> O God, I have an ill-divining soul!
> Methinks I see thee, now thou art below,
> As one dead in the bottom of a tomb.

These hints of tragedy increase the suspense (and the irony) of the play (see also pp. 42-43).

Yet now and again the rush and hurry, the dread and confusion stop, and there shines forth a tender beauty, appropriately enough in scenes of still moonlight—"That tips with silver all these fruit-tree tops".

It is significant that there are no fewer than eleven operas based on *Romeo and Juliet* (the most popular one by Gounod). The reason is obvious—there are so many different emotional shades, such variety in tone colours.

Most of Shakespeare's tragedies end on a note of hope, and this, the first, strikes the pattern of the rest. The lives of these lovers are burnt up, but the final effect of the play is not wholly pessimistic. It would have been had their deaths *increased* the hatred of the Montagues and Capulets. But at the end the heads of these two houses shake hands over the "poor sacrifices of their enmity". The tragedy has left things better than they were at the start of the play.

Setting

The great majority of Shakespeare's scenes (apart from those in the Histories) are set in places abroad, a device which of itself gave them a romantic colouring. But the local colour of all his plays is that of Elizabethan England, whether the story is one of Italy, Egypt or Denmark, and in whatever age. Nowadays we should demand strict accuracy in scenery, costumes and topical references, but then, for playwright and audience alike, the life and spirit of a play mattered more than strict accuracy in local colour. "It is the spirit which giveth life." People saw in the drama a reflection of their own life and experience; its appeal was in no wise analytical or educational, but human

Further, in those days people were untravelled and uneducated, and anachronisms would not strike a false note in an age more familiar with stories than with their setting. Only a very few privileged persons could know (by travel or study) what Italian cities were really like, so that the incongruity of the local colour would pass unnoticed.

And it must be remembered that there was no scenery and no period costume. Incongruities which become apparent beside "realistic" scenery would not be noticed then. In references to a character's dress it would be farcical were the references historically correct but to something the character was not actually wearing on the stage!

Romeo and Juliet takes place nominally in Verona (one scene in Mantua). Although pomegranate trees and ducats are mentioned, we are really never very far from the England Shakespeare knew. The local colour is essentially Elizabethan.

When trouble is afoot in the streets the cry is "Clubs, bills, and partisans!"; "Clubs!" being the shout of London apprentices seeking reinforcements in their street brawls or their rallying cry for attack.

Capulet is represented as "the great rich Capulet", but his household is that of a regular Elizabethan lord of the manor—small enough, indeed, for Lord and Lady to be at hand immediately the Nurse calls them from their daughter's bedroom. The kitchen staff is unable to cope with a great occasion, and the Nurse helps in the pantry and the Lord stops up all night and sees that there are enough dry logs for the fire. The Lady has in her own keeping the key to the cupboard where expensive things like spices are kept. The masque (masked dance) was very popular at the time *Romeo and Juliet* was written and had not yet developed into the more ambitious type of entertainment it became later in Shakespeare's life under the patronage of James I. The dance is held in the same hall as the supper. After "trenchers", "joint-stools" and "plate" have been cleared away, the tables are "turned up", more torches are called for and the fire is quenched (see note on "quench the fire", p. 65), as "the room is grown too hot". Then the dancers begin to "tickle *the senseless rushes* with their heels".

On the wedding morning the bridegroom is to go early to awake the bride with music and take her to church for the ceremony, the Elizabethan way of doing things.

Wandering minstrels (as distinct from musicians) are of low repute in Elizabethan England: in these days of printing their services are of little account, and it is considered an insult to a man to imply that he belongs to such a class (III. i). The speediest method of travel is by hiring post-horses. In time of "infectious pestilence" the doors of houses where it "reigns" are "seal'd up". This was the constable's duty in Shakespearean England, and everyone in the theatre would remember how the theatres were closed on account of the plague in 1593-1594—assuming *Romeo and Juliet* to be written after this date (see p. 7). The muddle-headed zeal of the "Watch" (the regular term for the officers of Shakespeare's day) is a constant subject of satire in his plays; the watchman in charge here is of the same kith and kin as the "Watch" in other plays, diligently but unintelligently taking great pride in little duties, such men as had no doubt amused Shakespeare in the Stratford of his youth. The Apothecary's shop is thoroughly Elizabethan. Altogether the play gives as true a cross-section of Elizabethan life as any play on an avowedly contemporary topic.

There were no tombs such as that in Act V, Sc. iii, in Shakespeare's England. This massive vault is not due to a sudden desire for Italian local colour, however, it is simply that the scene could not be represented otherwise.

Some people say that the hot days and moonlight nights, and, above all, the impetuous passion, give the play an Italian setting. But are there no hot days and moonlight nights in England? As for full-blooded passion, in Shakespeare's plays this is by no means reserved for men and women of Italian, or any other, race.

Characters

Romeo

> Then plainly know my heart's dear love is set
> On the fair daughter of rich Capulet.

Before the start of the play Romeo has been moody and reserved. The lady whom he says he loves will have none of him. (So far as the construction of the play is concerned, the fact that Rosaline has no love for him means that he does not sacrifice the sympathy of the audience when he makes love to Juliet. He would appear a blackguard had he jilted her.) At the time the play opens he goes out at night and locks himself up all day. Perhaps his love is only wounded self-esteem. He fancies that he is in love, but his love is sentimental, not genuine; he has posed to be in love, and he cannot distinguish the pose from the real thing, and finally he has become in love, so far as he can tell. Thus his love is a production of his fancy, he is in love with being in love. The Friar points the difference between real love and Romeo's.

> *Romeo.* Thou chid'st me oft for loving Rosaline.
> *Friar Laurence.* For doting, not for loving, pupil mine.

He enjoys airing his misfortunes, like people who love to talk about their ailments. But he does not talk of love in a deep and sincere way. He trifles with clever, but unconvincing, antitheses, *e.g.*

> Here's much to do with hate, but more with love.
> Why, then, O brawling love! O loving hate!
> O any thing, of nothing first create!
> O heavy lightness! serious vanity!
> Mis-shapen chaos of well-seeming forms!
> Feather of lead, bright smoke, cold fire, sick health!
> Still-waking sleep, that is not what it is!
> This love feel I, that feel no love in this.

When he is really in love, he keeps it to himself. As the Friar said, his love "did read by rote and could not spell" —there was little meaning behind his words. He cultivates a melancholy detachment from life.

> Tut, I have lost myself; I am not here;
> This is not Romeo, he's some other where.

But Romeo has not always been like this. It is only lately that he has become a dreamer. The very fact that his companions make so much of his changed "humour" shows that he must have been a jolly fellow in the days gone by. The head of a rival house pays tribute to the esteem in which he is held.

> He bears him like a portly gentleman;
> And, to say truth, Verona brags of him
> To be a virtuous and well-govern'd youth.

Everything goes to show that Romeo was naturally a charming young man, a good "mixer", with plenty of friends, leading an active life. His father is glad that he was not near the street affray. We see why later on, for he turns out to be an excellent swordsman. When love really gets to his heart, life is real; his love is the most important thing to him, and as a consequence he enjoys everything in life all the more, he lives to a higher power, so to speak. "Now art thou sociable, *now art thou Romeo*," says Mercutio, which is the last word upon the matter.

It is arranged by his friends that he should go to the Capulet masque in order to meet ladies fairer than Rosaline. One might have supposed that such purpose would have *increased* his determination to prove Rosaline the best, as he himself says,

> I'll go along, no such sight to be shown,
> But to rejoice in splendour of mine own.

It is in face of this determination that he loses his heart to Juliet, which shows the impact that she made upon him.

> Did my heart love till now? forswear it, sight!
> For I ne'er saw true beauty till this night.

His speeches now are full of real emotion, beautiful and imaginative. He shows that he has the heart of a poet. His actions have purpose; he risks death to see Juliet, though even now he is much given to talk. Romeo's is a less practical nature than Juliet's. Casting care to the winds he will marry Juliet forthwith, but she has to remind him that he will have to make arrangements for the wedding and provides means for him to let her know what they are, while he is wondering if it is all a dream. Romeo is meditating

> It is my soul that calls upon my name:
> How silver-sweet sound lovers' tongues by night,
> Like softest music to attending ears!

but Juliet calls him back to present realities—

> *Juliet.*   At what o'clock to-morrow
> Shall I send to thee?
> > *Romeo.*   At the hour of nine.
> > *Juliet.* I will not fail.

So Romeo goes to the Friar standing "on sudden haste", a man of purpose, but no organiser. Then he ceases to brood upon his love before his friends, and instead of making them miserable he meets them in their own mood.

When Tybalt comes seeking his blood Romeo acts as a peacemaker and as a gentleman. He tries to calm him down, and it would appear to be not without difficulty that he keeps his sword at his side. Yet he does so, and he still refuses to draw his sword when refusal looks like cowardice, and he is not concerned about what his friend Mercutio thinks of him. But the death of Mercutio, his life-long friend, at Tybalt's hand is too much for Romeo, and once roused beyond the point that he can bear he has no thought for consequences. "Fire-eyed fury be my conduct now." This is Romeo all through.

After banishment at a stroke has changed Romeo's outlook from one of joy to one of misery, he shows his temperamental nature to less advantage. Before Juliet he spoke and acted like a man: before the Friar he acts like a spoilt child, throwing himself on the ground and tearing his hair in a frenzy. Such a lack of self-control is pitiable. There is only one way of escape—suicide. He is utterly unmanned, and had Juliet seen him now she would at least have been shocked and it would not have been surprising had she regretted her "faithful vow" to marry him. He bandies the word "banished" about in his talk just as before he had done the word "love". It is the words and poise of the Friar, not his own manliness and self-control, which bring him to himself and decide his course of action.

Escaping from Juliet's room next morning he is a man again, though still changeable, deciding to go, to stay, and, finally, to go, though it must be allowed that his changes of mood were at the call of Juliet.

Still impetuous in banishment he believes the first thing he hears, without a question as to how and why. His action again is purposeful but hasty, as if he must do *something*, but cannot wait to consider if it is for the best. This time, however, he acts like a man, not like a child: there is no moaning and grovelling, he gives curt, decisive commands. So he gets the means for suicide by Juliet's body and rushes off "in post" to the Capulet tomb, paying no attention to what his man says on the way.

> What said my man, when my betossed soul
> Did not attend him as we rode? I think
> He told me Paris should have married Juliet:
> Said he not so? or did I dream it so?
> Or am I mad, hearing him talk of Juliet,
> To think it was so?

It comes as a surprise that he stops to write a letter to his father before he goes, and is much to his credit.

The irony of it is that had he been in less of a hurry all would have been well. When he has killed Paris (remember that it was Paris who first offered fight), he says that Paris is "One writ with me in sour misfortune's book". Romeo was indeed unlucky, and the enmity between the Montagues and Capulets was none of his doing, but, although there is not so strict a connection between character and events as in Shakespeare's later tragedies (it is difficult to see how there could be in a course of events lasting only five days), there is not a little relation between Romeo's headstrong haste and the events of Act V. The tragedy was far from a "work of heaven".

Romeo appears at his best just before his death. He has killed a man who, rejecting fair words of peace, went on to seek his life—it must have been one or other of them. But he has no words of bitterness for him and takes his hand and lays him gently "in a triumphant grave". (Bear in mind, however, that Romeo had no certain knowledge of the projected marriage between Paris and Juliet.)

As we look on Romeo for the last time, his so short-lived happiness in dust and ashes, we feel an infinite sympathy for him as he shakes "the yoke of inauspicious stars from this world-wearied flesh". He had felt "the yoke of inauspicious stars" from the first, since he set out to the masque where he first met Juliet.

> I fear, too early: for my mind misgives
> Some consequence yet hanging in the stars
> Shall bitterly begin his fearful date
> With this night's revels and expire the term
> Of a despised life closed in my breast
> By some vile forfeit of untimely death.

Even in the hour of marriage he had a feeling that his joy was only a shaft of sunlight through a dark sky—

> Do thou but close our hands with holy words,
> Then love-devouring death do what he dare.

And so it was.

Juliet

Romeo . . . take all myself.

When we first meet Juliet she is a charming girlish creature, an obedient daughter willing to marry anyone of whom mother approves.

> But no more deep will I endart mine eye
> Than your consent gives strength to make it fly.

She has apparently lived a conventional and sheltered family life, but when she falls in love she becomes resolute and unflinching and passionate—no one else can think for her here. All at once she is a woman with a mind of her own, willing to stand up against mother, father and all the world. There is more development in her character than in Romeo's, and this development is one of the things that make the play seem to take longer than the five days allowed (see p. 10).

Her resource and determination at the age of thirteen make one wonder whether Shakespeare had had much to do with children. On the stage hers is no child's part.

She falls in love with Romeo at first sight, and after that has one purpose. She is more matter-of-fact and practical than he, and dreams over things less.

> How camest thou hither, tell me, and wherefore?
> The orchard walls are high and hard to climb,
> And the place death, considering who thou art.

Romeo's

> With love's light wings did I o'er-perch these walls;
> For stony limits cannot hold love out.

fails to convince her, and she continues, "If they do see thee, they will murder thee"; her next two remarks are similarly practical, while Romeo is indulging in flights of fancy. Romeo wonders if it is all a dream.

> I am afeard,
> Being in night, all this is but a dream,
> Too flattering-sweet to be substantial.

She gives sensible directions which lead somewhere.

> If that thy bent of love be honourable,
> Thy purpose marriage, send me word to-morrow,
> By one that I'll procure to come to thee,
> Where and what time thou wilt perform the rite.

Later on, when Romeo is musing, she breaks in with a matter-of-fact reminder that they have not fixed a time for her messenger to come to Romeo on the morrow (see p. 20). Juliet loves Romeo well, but her feet are on the earth. She is not forward, however, and feels embarrassed when Romeo overhears her avowal of love, and, indeed, gets a bit flustered (see the speech beginning, "Thou know'st the mask of night is on my face").

When she hears of Tybalt's death the whole background of her life so far displaces her love for Romeo, but not for long. She soon springs to his defence when her nurse blames Romeo. *She* can blame her Romeo, but let anyone else do so! None the less, Romeo's action does not seem to make sense, then, by a womanly intuition, it all comes to her—"That villain cousin would have kill'd my husband". His banishment is a worse blow, she says, than the death of father or mother, which should not be taken too literally, as here she is greatly affected and is speaking wildly, although most newly-married girls, it is to be supposed, would sooner lose parents than husband. All is understood, and Juliet bids him "come to take his last farewell". On their last appearance alive together her alternate wishes for him to stay a little longer and to be gone for his own safety are very true to life.

Henceforward she must play a part. John Masefield says that she becomes "a deceitful, scheming liar".* This is certainly not Shakespeare's reading of her character, nor that of any producer of *Romeo and Juliet* up to now. She cannot be true to parents *and* true to Romeo, and who shall condemn her for first loyalty to husband? She was, at all events, no more deceitful than the Friar, whom Masefield considers one of those "calm, wise, gentle people who speak largely, from a vision detached from the world".

It can be said that Juliet was selfish, giving her family great worry in order to carry through her own whims and fancies. This might be the reading of events of the Forsyte family, it was not Shakespeare's. *Romeo and Juliet* has the thrill of young love from the point of view of the young lovers. Juliet loved her father and mother with a dutiful affection, nothing more: she loved Romeo with all her heart and soul. He is away, she is left alone,

* *Shakespeare*, Williams & Norgate.

and those who are nearest seek to force her into an unwilling marriage. Her father, anxious for his daughter to marry into the royal family, cuts her off with

> An you be mine, I'll give you to my friend;
> An you be not, hang, beg, starve, die in the streets.

She turns to her mother,

> O, sweet my mother, cast me not away!
> Delay this marriage for a month, a week:

but all she gets is

> Talk not to me, for I'll not speak a word:
> Do as thou wilt, for I *have done with thee.*

Then to the Nurse, but there she finds only worldly wisdom.

> Then, since the case so stands as now it doth,
> I think it best you married with the county.
> O, he's a lovely gentleman!
> Romeo's a dishclout to him.
>
> I think you are happy in this second match,
> For it excels your first: or if it did not,
> Your first is dead; or 'twere as good he were,
> As living here and you no use of him.

It is obvious that she can expect no help here, and with an exhausted sarcasm she gives up—"Well, thou hast comforted me marvellous much". After the Nurse has gone she lets fly.

> Ancient damnation! O most wicked fiend!
> Thou and my bosom henceforth shall be twain.

Like Romeo, she thinks that life is very hard and blames an outside hand.

> Alack, alack, that heaven should practise stratagems
> Upon so soft a subject as myself!

She, too, has her premonition of an ugly fate overhanging their love, which is perhaps more to do with the suspense and foreboding in the atmosphere of the play than with her character in particular.

> O God, I have an ill-divining soul!
> Methinks I see thee, now thou art below,
> As one dead in the bottom of a tomb.

She has nothing against Paris *as a person*, and treats him politely at Friar Laurence's cell, and, of course, it would be unwise to arouse suspicion by ignoring him. She feigns compliance before old Capulet, and acts well enough to hoodwink him completely. Her glad acceptance of the Friar's "remedy" shows her extreme courage. "O, tell not me of fear!" she says. But, as night creeps on and the hour to take the drug approaches, the risks of her situation bring horrific pictures to her mind as she is alone in her room. "A faint cold fear thrills through her veins" and horrid images pass before her mind's eye. Life is sweet, life is pleasant: the tomb is frightening. By his unwholesome imagery Shakespeare here conveys her feeling; we project ourselves into the being of Juliet and live her life. The thought of waking in a tomb is terrifying to contemplate and her language has a compelling intensity: but with a waking dream that Romeo is in danger she drinks the drug to him—"Romeo, I come! this do I drink to thee". By an unlucky chapter of accidents she never sees him alive again. But leave him she will not. The Friar cannot hustle her away from him, even in death. And when she hears the noise of people approaching she no doubt realises (she was always practical) that now, with Romeo dead, she will have no choice but to marry Paris. There is still one way out. She had said that "If all else fail, myself have power to die". It was no empty boast. The love that had thrilled her life now ends it.

> O happy dagger!
> This is thy sheath; there rust and let me die.

In common with all Shakespeare's tragic heroines, at the moment of stress Juliet has only herself to rely on—"My dismal scene I needs must act alone". The dramatic effect of this is to throw them on their own resources—they have no one else to turn to, and this awakens sympathy for their lonely hand and increases the pathos of their situation. Juliet can depend neither on Romeo (for he is banished), on father, mother nor nurse (see p. 25).

Mercutio

A gentleman, nurse, that loves to hear himself talk,
and will speak more in a minute than he will stand to
in a month.

Mercutio is important in so far as he affects Romeo, not
for himself. Dramatically he is a character-contrast with
Romeo. Everywhere he goes he provides comic relief of a
witty and intelligent kind (instead of a "low" kind like
that of the musicians). He is a mere name in Brooke's poem
and Painter's story (see pp. 10-11), but in Shakespeare's
play he becomes a living person with an interest of his own.

He is hearty and lively, one of the hail-fellow-well-met
type, a good mixer, the sort of man who makes any party
go with a swing, but who gets on your nerves, maybe, when
you have to live with him day after day. He is a gay and
incorrigible chatterbox, full of sheer animal spirits, what
now we call a "bright spark", a "live wire". Naturally,
such a man regards Romeo's "humour" as a dreary flop
and tries to do something to liven him up. Such men
imagine that they are the life and soul of the party and
they want everyone to know it: they do brighten up things
in small doses, but invariably keep on and on and make
everybody bored—or angry. Men are not disposed to have
their troubles laughed away by somebody to whom they
mean nothing—"He jests at scars that never felt a wound".
He is an exuberant character, whipping up the pace of the
play. A chatterbox he may be, but not an *empty* chatterbox, and much of what he says is very witty and full of
shrewd sense. He loves a joke—a questionable joke as well
as any. He likes to shock people. He is an expert in
wilfully misinterpreting people's words, and fancies himself as a maker of puns and a jester with the meaning of
words. His fun is always good-humoured and never
unkind, save perhaps when he makes fun of the Nurse's
looks (II. iv), a matter on which women are very touchy,
though even here much would depend on the tone of voice
in which his remarks were said.

He will not be persuaded to peace by Benvolio and whips
up enmity with his tongue. "Make it a word and a blow"
is his challenge to Tybalt as soon as he comes along.
Mercutio is not one to fight with words only. He loves a
fight of any kind, and is not only prepared but wants to

defend what he considers to be the honour of his set with
sword if need be, and draws the fight upon himself when
his friend seems too cowardly.

> O calm, dishonourable, vile submission!
> Alla stoccata carries it away.
> Tybalt, you rat-catcher, will you walk?

After he is "sped", "A plague o' both your houses!" he
cries (three times), but he has only himself to thank.   He
has got what he asked for.   He meets death as he had met
life, with a jest—"Ask for me to-morrow, and you shall
find me a grave man".

The dramatic reason for Mercutio's death is that Romeo
shall have a compelling reason for killing Tybalt, an offence
serious enough to result in banishment.   Further, Mercutio
was getting more attention than Romeo, therefore he must
be disposed of or the interest of the play would be where
the dramatist did not want it.   In the original story the
death of Mercutio is not mentioned: it is Shakepeare's
invention to make a better play.

There is another side to the character of this chatterbox
whose humour was not always in the best taste.   This same
man has music in his soul and beauty in his mind.   His
description of Queen Mab (I. iv) shows his quick imagination,

> Nothing but vain fantasy,
> Which is as thin of substance as the air
> And more inconstant than the wind.

It is in the nature of those who like to be prominent in
company to take after the latest fashion, in order to be
noticed.   But not so Mercutio.

> The plague of such antic, lisping, affecting fantasticoes;
> these new tuners of accents!   "By Jesu, a very good
> blade! a very tall man! a very good wench!"   Why, is
> not this a lamentable thing, grandsire, that we should be
> thus afflicted with these strange flies, these fashion-
> mongers, these *pardonnez-mois*, who stand so much on
> the new form, that they cannot sit at ease on the old
> bench?   O, their *bons*, their *bons!*

This shows how Shakespeare creates individuals, not mere
types.

The Nurse

Ancient damnation!

The Nurse occupies the same position in relation to Juliet as Mercutio in relation to Romeo. Like him she is Shakespeare's creation from a mere hint. Juliet relies upon her more than upon her mother, indeed, in the play the Nurse is a more important person than Juliet's mother and her own mistress. Dramatically her common nature is a contrast to Juliet's tenderness and dignity, her superficiality to Juliet's love and devotion. Her contribution to the comic relief of the play is discussed elsewhere (p. 13).

Coarse and vulgar, of the earth earthy, the Nurse is a woman of no education or refinement or taste. It is surprising that Juliet is so ladylike when her breeding has been in charge of this woman, but it seems to have been a belief of Shakespeare's (generally in the plays, not specifically here) that birth will out whatever the breeding (*e.g. Cymbeline*). In giving a message she has the irrelevance of the uneducated, the failure to spot the thing that matters and keep to it. She is very wordy and takes nearly five minutes to say how old Juliet is (I. iii), and nearly as long to tell Romeo what she has come for (II. iv). She speaks much and says little. She enjoys having people hanging upon her words—"What she bade me say, I will keep to myself"; she likes having a bit of power over people, and in II. v she keeps Juliet waiting as long as she can for Romeo's message; and when she has to tell her young mistress that Romeo is banished (III. ii) she torments her with hints in clumsy fashion before she gets it across. Then she keeps the essential information to the end (III. ii. 129).

She does not really care for Juliet, hers is a possessive kind of affection that likes to have her in her power (I. iii. 2-3). She prides herself on her position and has an undue sense of her own importance—"I nursed her daughter, that you talk'd withal". She likes to gain praise by impressing on Juliet what she owes to her—"I am the drudge and toil in your delight". She enjoys ordering Peter about—the servant is a regular snob in the way she treats *her* servant.

None the less the Nurse has a position of trust in the family with whom she has been for so long. She is a servant of some importance, with a "man" to wait upon her and give her escort. The family rely upon her. When there is a rush she helps out in the kitchen or wherever required. Shakespeare had seen (or met) family servants like this in the big houses of Warwickshire. She has a careless freedom in speech, but she knows on which side her bread is buttered and always takes her lead from the family. She echoes Lady Capulet's praise of Paris.

Lady Capulet.   Verona's summer hath not such a flower.
Nurse.   Nay, he's a flower; in faith, a very flower.

Next morning she is doing as she is bid to hasten the marriage of her young mistress to Romeo. In the afternoon, when her mistress curses Romeo, the Nurse at once echoes her—"Shame come to Romeo". But when her mistress's mood veers round so does her own, and she offers to find him and fetch him—"Hark ye, your Romeo will be here at night". When Juliet is saying good-bye to Romeo she gives warning of her mother's approach. When she imagines that, after all, Juliet has decided to marry Paris, round swings the weather-cock again—"O, he's a lovely gentleman! Romeo's a dishclout to him"; and all in the day's work she goes to waken Juliet for a wedding to a second husband. Only when Death steps in can she speak without a cue: there is but one response.

The Nurse is far from an attractive character. Yet she has something to recommend her. Juliet entrusts her with all her secrets and has no fear but that they will be kept. She does not even make the Nurse promise secrecy, she takes it for granted. Yet the Nurse is the sort of person who finds it hard to keep a secret and loves to be the bearer of news. This shows that so far the Nurse had always been faithful to her. Until the Nurse turns against Romeo, Juliet trusts her to the full.

Beshrew my very heart,
I think you are happy in this second match,
For it excels your first.

Such worldly wisdom little sorts with Juliet's high ideal of love. The help that Juliet needs now it is beyond her to give. She thinks of her own advantage in the eyes of her lord and lady, and "makes the best of a bad job" when she advises Juliet to marry Paris. The propriety or morality of being married to two men at once does not enter her mind; she is all for expediency.

There is no doubt that she is fond of Juliet. She sticks up for her against her father when he is so angry with her.

> God in heaven bless her!
> You are to blame, my lord, to rate her so.

Even her advice to Juliet to throw over Romeo was probably dictated by what she thought to be the best for her.

Altogether she is a bundle of contradictions—and in that alone a more human character. Coleridge's summary of her character is worth quoting.

> The garrulity of age* strengthened by the feelings of a long-trusted servant, whose sympathy with the mother's affections gives her privileges in the household; and observe . . . the childlike fondness of repetition . . . and also that happy, humble, ducking under, yet constant resurgence against, the check of her superiors!

It has already been pointed out how the fact that Juliet has this vulgar old woman for company throws her on her own resources in the moment of trial (p. 26).

Capulet

> You are too hot.

Capulet is much older than his wife. She is under thirty, but old Capulet is "past his dancing days" and it is thirty years since he went masking (I. v). He says in another place (I. ii) that it is not hard "For men so old as we to keep the peace". However, he is not too old to stop up all night.

His character is not consistent. In I. ii he is a loving father. "The earth hath swallow'd all my hopes but she," he says, with a touch of pathos. He is not disposed to determine his daughter's choice of husband (I. ii. 16-17), and he does not wish Paris to marry her unless he loves her (32-33). In any case he must wait for two years.

He enjoys entertaining and is proud of his guests.

> At my poor house look to behold this night
> Earth-treading stars that make dark heaven light.

He tries to make people welcome, greeting them with little pleasantries, and even when he feels tired and wants to go to bed he cheerfully says the conventional "*Must* you

* She could not, however, have been more than about fifty-five (see I. iii).

go?" of the Elizabethan host—"Is it e'en so?". He wishes
to avoid any cause of disturbance at his party and makes
Tybalt know his place when he seeks to "make a mutiny
among his guests". He would that the Montagues were
made as welcome as anyone else. There is a fragrance
about the character of a man who can think in such terms
as these.

> Let two more summers wither in their pride,
> Ere we may think her ripe to be a bride.

> Such comfort as do lusty young men feel
> When well-apparell'd April on the heel
> Of limping winter treads.

But in Act III "the great rich Capulet" is a petty squire
furious beyond measure when his daughter crosses him and
refuses to marry a kinsman of the royal family at once.
Lady Capulet knows how he will take Juliet's refusal.

> Here comes your father; tell him so yourself,
> And see how he will take it at your hands.

He takes it in a way not unlike that of the Tybalt whom
he censures and restrains in I. v. In later tragedies Shakespeare would not have made a character inconsistent in
order to fit him into the plot (in this case to force Juliet's
decision to take the Friar's potion). Capulet fails to consider her wish, as the Capulet of I. ii—apparently sincerely
—intended. The Capulet who told Paris that he must wait
two years now says that he can marry her in a matter of
days. It is a wonder that Paris is not suspicious about
the sudden change of front. He talks about giving his
"decree" to his daughter, and roughly gives her orders to
marry Paris in ungentlemanly terms.

> Thank me no thankings, nor proud me no prouds,
> But fettle your fine joints 'gainst Thursday next.

He is soon in a violent temper, heaping various terms of
abuse upon her, and he can hardly keep his hands off her
("My fingers itch"). He imposed his will on Tybalt at
his first party, but in a firmer, more dignified and less
ranting way. When the Nurse sticks up for Juliet he rates
her too. He considers Juliet now as his property to place
where he will.

> An you be mine, I'll give you to my friend;
> An you be not, hang, beg, starve, die in the streets,
> For, by my soul, I'll ne'er acknowledge thee,
> Nor what is mine shall never do thee good:
> Trust to't, bethink you; *I'll not be forsworn.*

No doubt he would consider that he was just in controlling a headstrong girl—"How now, my headstrong!". How headstrong Juliet was we know full well from her sudden and intense love of Romeo.

Hasty and uncontrollable though he be in his anger at what he considers Juliet's petulance, yet he has some care for her. His scheme to marry her is based on what he considers best for her. As the Friar says,

> The most you sought was her promotion;
> For 'twas your heaven she should be advanced.

But Capulet's love of her is a possessive love, like that of the Nurse (see p. 29). He loves her because she belongs to him, as a man loves his horse or, in these days, his car. His view of marriage is entirely material, the man with the best title (or purse) is the one to marry.

He is quite selfish. The wedding must be hurried on before Juliet changes her mind (very different from his counsel of delay in I. ii). In view of Tybalt's death it would be fitting to have a quiet wedding—"no great ado, a friend or two", but he wants to be "proper" and soon forgets about this and prepares for a feast needing "twenty cunning cooks". His grief for Tybalt is purely conventional and superficial, and he comments on his death with a trivial platitude—"Well, we were born to die". He overrides Juliet's (supposed) grief by a drastic decree that she shall be married in spite of all. His forced metaphors when he finds Juliet crying (III. v) show his insincere nature. He will have his own way at all costs. He treats his wife like a child, and on an important occasion takes the affairs of the kitchen out of her hands—"Let me alone; I'll play the housewife for this once". Such a man can see only his own point of view. He can see the failures of his inferiors, but nothing but success can spring from his own efforts, a weakness common to those in authority. When things are, as he thinks, going well and Juliet has consented to marry Paris, he arranges the wedding for the next day, in order to make doubly sure. His wife knows how this will affect arrangements already made, but he lightly and dogmatically passes over her objection.

> Tush, I will stir about,
> And all things shall be well, I warrant thee, wife.

It is not surprising that Juliet could have little regard for a father like this, who alternately cursed and petted her. She could have no sense of reliance upon and trust in him. (But the father of Act I, Sc. ii, would be worth her devotion.) Whatever his affection for his daughter, he failed to understand her. This is mentioned as a matter of fact, not of condemnation: there are many fathers who fail to understand their daughters.

All the same, it is pathetic when she is taken from him, just when his heart was "wondrous light". "And with my child my joys are buried," he says.

At the end it is he who first holds out his hand to Montague and seeks to make reparation for the waste of young lives their quarrel has made.

Capulet's character is important as a background only. The connection of his character with the action of the play is that there shall be a compelling necessity for Juliet to trust herself to the Friar's "remedy".

Lady Capulet

> Well, think of marriage now.

Lady Capulet is even more anxious than her husband that Juliet should not miss the chance of marriage to a royal Count, even more mercenary in her view of marriage —"So shall you share all that he doth possess". She is weaker and more slightly drawn than he, and says little original. Perhaps this is not surprising in the young wife of a much older man: she is about twenty-eight (I. iii. 52-53), and he, it would appear, about sixty. Apparently she is not greatly attached to him: at any rate her first words remind him of his age in none too kindly fashion. She follows his lead none the less, and when she is left to herself she cannot make up her mind, at one moment telling the Nurse to go, at the next to stay. When she speaks of her own "old age" (V. iii. 205-206) it is questionable whether she exaggerates or whether Shakespeare was again careless and inconsistent. Ideas of age are, of course, relative.

Lady Capulet is "old" compared to Juliet who now lies dead, but even so it is unlikely that a mother of under thirty would think of referring to her "old age". This is another instance of the *impression* of the play being different from the *facts* of the play (see pp. 9-10).

When she first praises Paris her metaphors are very ordinary, not to say far-fetched (her long speech in I. iii), and this emphasises that she is a very ordinary person. She is not so fiery and testy as her husband, but more implacable and bitter—though not to Juliet. Her desire for revenge for Tybalt's murder outweighs her grief for his loss. She calls on the Prince for vengeance.

> Prince, as thou art true,
> For blood of ours, shed blood of Montague.

As she ironically says to Juliet,

> Well, girl, thou weep'st not so much for his death,
> As that the villain lives which slaughter'd him.

Much grief, she says, "shows still some want of wit". She has never felt deeply about anything: she has lived on the surface, and the routine of every day supplies her trivial interests in life. But she is determined on vengeance, the resort of a little nature—"We will have vengeance for it, fear thou not"—and plans to have Romeo poisoned "That he shall soon keep Tybalt company". Obviously she would stop at nothing.

She has no more community of feeling with her daughter than her husband has. Lacking understanding she lacks sympathy, and is petty and vindictive when Juliet will not marry whom she wishes—"I would the fool were married to her grave!" and "Do as thou wilt, for I have done with thee". It would be silly, however, to take these remarks literally. In moments of impatience we all make hasty speeches which we should not stand to seriously if every word were to be weighed. When "the fool" *is* "in her grave", however, it is to be noticed that her first thought is how it affects *herself*.

> O me, O me! My child, *my only life*,
> Revive, look up, *or I will die with thee!*

> But one, poor one, one poor and loving child,
> But one thing to rejoice and solace in,
> And *cruel death hath catch'd it from my sight!*

Friar Laurence

We still have known thee for a holy man.

Everyone speaks well of the Friar, a steadying influence in a stormy world of suddenly changing passions. He is plain and homely, ready to give help where it is needed. He means well; it is a pity that his plans work out so ill. He is a theorist, inexperienced in the practical world of men.

His speeches are grave, sometimes sombre. They carry weight and authority, and rhyme lends the effect of a chant to his first utterances. They are often beautiful, for example his opening words describing the way "the frowning night" gives way to "grey-eyed morn". It is in the nature of his profession to moralise. He can be powerful, and soon brings Romeo to his senses when he is in a frenzy.

But his monastic seclusion is of little help in the affairs of an active world. He tries to comfort a young man just married who has been banished the country by "adversity's sweet milk philosophy". Young lovers are impatient of an old man's advice. He would be true to all at the same time, but when their interests run contrary to one another it is impossible. He cannot keep silence about Romeo and Juliet and be faithful, or even fair, to her parents or Count Paris. He has been Romeo's spiritual father from his childhood and does not like to disappoint his charge. He consents to marry him in the hope, he persuades himself, that the two families will be reconciled; in other words, he fails in his duty for an ultimate good. He *hopes* for the best, rather than fears for the worst. He is well-meaning, but not very sensible. However, it is easy for us to be wise after the event. Perhaps it is owing to his good intentions that he cannot see how he is to blame and lays the catastrophe at the feet of "heaven".

We may call him false for conducting a secret marriage and advising a young bride what lies to tell to her unwitting parents when she gets back home. He is certainly just as deceitful as Juliet. But this Galsworthian reading of the character, carefully weighing right and wrong, is not Shakespeare's intention. This would be to let logic take the place of the tone and feeling of the play. Shakespeare probably just dramatised the old story without thinking of all the

implications of the Friar's consent to be Romeo's accom-
plice. Put simply—the Friar is on Romeo's side and so
we sympathise with him, and Shakespeare arranges the
play thus.

The dramatic reasons for the Friar's character are to provide a contrast to Romeo and Juliet, and a person skilled
in herbal properties, as the source of the potion which was
to send Juliet to a living death. Many of his speeches are
very long for their dramatic purpose, for instance, the first
one, which is necessary only to show his knowledge of
herbs, so that we are prepared for his unusual skill and
later on do not reject the potion he gives Juliet as an
incredible fiction.

It is strange that since the Friar is so well spoken of he is
not ready at the tomb in good time for Juliet's awaking
after a sleep of forty-two hours—about four o'clock on the
Friday afternoon—but then there would have been no play.

The Friar speaks of himself as a very old man (V. iii.
228-229), but this is probably exaggerated in the stress of
the moment. He is not too old to manage "lantern, crow
and spade"; he stumbles, it is true, amid the gravestones,
but then it is dark. The Prince speaks as if he has known
him for a long time, and the general impression is that he
is an old, but not a very old, man.

Tybalt

What, drawn, and talk of peace! I hate the word.

We first meet Tybalt rushing in to stir up a fight: the
last we see of him is when he is killed in one. Between the
two he talks of nothing but fighting and never speaks other
than angrily.

He is a mischief-maker, quick to take offence, quick to
provoke incidents. He jumps to conclusions, assuming
that Romeo has come to the mask to make trouble (I. v.
60-61). Capulet's tribute to a foe he cannot grasp, calls
Romeo a villain out of hand and says that he'll "not
endure him". His inflammable nature chooses to take it
as a personal affront that Romeo should come to his uncle's
mask; really it was none of his business, especially as he
was a junior in the family. Put in his place by his uncle
he goes off in dudgeon and thinks that it is up to him to

keep the supposed insult alive and avenge it as soon as possible. Quarrels are the breath of life to him. Such people are very annoying and very difficult to get rid of.

"He's the courageous captain of compliments." He fancies himself mightily, and talks and fights according to the latest craze among up-to-date men of fashion. All men like to shine at something. Such men as he have no brains or good sense to recommend them, and so try to impress their fellows by their unrivalled prowess in brawling and fighting—the sort who say, "Let him try it on with *me! I'll* show him!"

Dramatically his appearance, or disappearance, is necessary in order to supply the reason for Romeo's banishment.

Benvolio

I do but keep the peace.

Romeo's cousin Benvolio is the reverse of Tybalt—a peace-maker from the very start.

Part, fools!
Put up your swords; you know not what you do.

He evades trouble—prevention is better than cure.

I pray thee, good Mercutio, let's retire:
The day is hot, the Capulets abroad,
And, if we meet, we shall not scape a brawl;
For now, these hot days, is the mad blood stirring.

He is not afraid of using his sword, however, but he prefers to use it to stop a fight rather than to make one. He tries to get Romeo out of the way before the Prince comes.

Stand not amazed: the prince will doom thee death,
If thou art taken: hence, be gone, away!

He believes in "safety first". When Mercutio says that he is "full of quarrels", he is, of course, speaking in humorous sarcasm—the opposite of the truth. Indeed, Mercutio often makes fun by sarcastically saying the opposite of what is true. Similarly, Mercutio calls him a "grand-sire"—his jocular way of saying that he is very serious. He is neither so forward in jesting as his friends, nor so quick to see a joke. This is not to say that he is old-fashioned, however: like the other young men he wants to keep up with the times—"The date is out of such prolixity".

Benvolio is trusted by all who know him. When Mercutio is wounded, Benvolio is the first one to whom he turns for help. He is the one called upon to give Montague a considered account of what has been happening in the first street-brawl of the play, and he tells Lady Montague of the peculiar change in her son; the Prince listens as he gives a fair account of what occasioned the deaths of Mercutio and Tybalt. "This is the truth, or let Benvolio die." He says little except in long serious speeches.

Benvolio is a close friend of Romeo and feels sure that he can drag Romeo's secret out of him—"I'll know his grievance, or be much denied". And his plan for curing Romeo succeeds—more quickly than he could ever have hoped.

Dramatically Benvolio sets off the character of Romeo (and also the characters of Mercutio and Tybalt) by contrast. He passes from the play at the end of Act III, Sc. i, when Mercutio and Tybalt are dead and Romeo is banished.

Paris

One writ with me in sour misfortune's book!

Paris appears but little, yet he is in the background all the time. He is bound to be dull beside Romeo, or he would steal the interest from him. He can marry Juliet without upsetting family prejudices. He is a conventional type of lover, who is content to woo "through the proper channels". This, of course, is not to his discredit. He is not pushing—he politely leaves the Friar's cell as soon as he is asked. He is not *necessarily* less fond of Juliet because he is more decorous in his approach to her ("Poor soul, thy face is much abused with tears"). But he is surely going too far on his own initiative when he settles the marriage, and even the wedding-day, without mentioning it to his bride-to-be, though it has to be remembered that he is impelled by Juliet's father (IV. i. 2-3) and that the rights of daughters in those days were not so well defined. He may be fond of Juliet, but it is believable that as a husband he will treat her in a lordly, masterful, even if quiet, manner, paying little attention to her opinions—

"That may be must be, love, on Thursday next". She
will become part of his household or estate, so to speak—
"Thy face is mine, and thou hast slander'd it". His
marriage with Juliet, so far as she is concerned, would be
what the French call a "marriage de convenance", in
contrast to the real love match with Romeo.

Paris is no coward. He defies Romeo's "conjurations"
and dies trying to prevent "some villanous shame" being
done to the grave of the girl he had hoped to marry. This
is the best evidence of his love in the play. And in death
he pleads, like Romeo, to be laid with her.

The Prince

Then will I be general of your woes.

The Prince is more a symbol than a person. He stands
for law and order in a troubled state, and speaks with a
weighty and authoritative voice, perhaps a rhetorical one,
in his first speech. He is more important for getting others
to speak than for what he says himself. He makes three
short appearances when there is trouble, delivers judgment
and is gone. The rhyme in his speech at the end of Act III,
Sc. i has a clinching effect, as if there is no more to be said
upon the matter.

Style

Professor Dowden has an excellent summary of the
development of Shakespeare's style.

> In the earliest plays the language is sometimes as it were a
> dress put upon the thought—a dress ornamented with super-
> fluous care; the idea is at times hardly sufficient to fill out
> the language in which it is put; in the middle of plays (*Julius
> Cæsar* serves as an example) there seems a perfect balance and
> equality between the thought and its expression. In the latest
> plays this balance is disturbed by the preponderance or excess
> of the ideas over the means of giving them utterance. The
> sentences are close-packed; there are "rapid and abrupt turn-
> ings of thought, so quick that language can hardly follow fast
> enough; impatient activity of intellect and fancy, which, having
> once disclosed an idea, cannot wait to work it orderly out";
> "the language is sometimes alive with imagery".*

Romeo and Juliet is one of the earliest plays (the first
tragedy entirely Shakespeare's own work) and is marked

* *Shakspere Primer*, p. 37. (See footnote p. 7.)

by the characteristics of those plays which Professor Dowden notices.

It is very different from Shakespeare's later plays in containing so much rhyme, much of it alternate rhyme (see also p. 36). The introduction of the passages in sonnet form (*e.g.* the first words between Romeo and Juliet) is also an indication of an early play. The sonnet was, however, a recognised medium for the language of love in Elizabethan England and is, therefore, not unfitting in that particular place.

The normal line in Shakespeare's plays is a blank verse iambic pentameter. There is much variation, however, making the verse more interesting to listen to and the dialogue more adapted to different characters. But there is not so much variation in the lines of *Romeo and Juliet* as in those of the later plays, and most of the lines are end-stopped, another sign of an early play.

Graphic and figurative language abounds, and the richness, vividness and variety of the imagery is to be noted. Nowhere in Shakespeare is there more lovely poetry than in *Romeo and Juliet*, nowhere is there more warmth and beauty and tenderness than in Act II. The similes and metaphors have that sense of surprise and yet of fitness which characterises the imagery of a genius.

> So far from sounding and discovery,
> As is the bud bit with an envious worm,
> Ere he can spread his sweet leaves to the air,
> Or dedicate his beauty to the sun.

> Such comfort as do lusty young men feel
> When well-apparell'd April on the heel
> Of limping winter treads, even such delight
> Among fresh female buds shall you this night
> Inherit at my house.

The student should learn those that particularly appeal to him. Similes and metaphors suit the occasion. Romeo, "savage wild", says that he will "strew this hungry churchyard with thy limbs". The student should contrast the imagery of the metaphors in Romeo's last speech in the tomb with those when he is making love to Juliet (*e.g.* III. v. 7-10). Sometimes simile and metaphor succeed one another quickly or are interwoven in one conception, *e.g.* III. iii. 130-134. The metaphors of the Prince—officialdom—are more ordinary (*e.g.* V. iii. 220). Where Shakespeare makes his metaphors far-fetched it is for dramatic effect. Lady Capulet's comparison of Paris to a book sounds hollow and insincere. Paris's good qualities are no reason for her recommendation of him as a suitor. Similarly Capulet's comparison of Juliet's eyes with the sea sounds forced—he is not speaking from the heart, but just trying to make an impression on Juliet.

Not only is there beauty in the imagery of the poetry, but the sound of many passages comes "like softest music to attending ears" (notice the beautiful alliteration in this very passage, giving the "silver-sweet" sound of which it is speaking). Alliteration is often used with onomatopoeic effect, for example the deadness of the *d*'s in "Then love-devouring death do what he dare".

In Elizabethan times punning was extremely popular, and this kind of verbal trickery (what the Elizabethans would call "conceits") is very prevalent in Shakespeare's earlier plays, more so in *Romeo and Juliet* than in any other tragedy. Punning is second nature to nearly every character in the play. Much of the point of this witty repartee is lost on a modern audience, and to the reader it becomes tiresome: he thinks how clever it is for a while, but cannot stand so much of it, and wishes to

> Take our good meaning, for our judgement sits
> Five times in that ere once in our five wits.

Indeed, it is not necessary for the modern audience to understand the exact point of Mercutio's jokes, so long as the general fun and frolic and nonsense comes over. It may be necessary for the serious student anxious to pass an examination, however. The play opens with puns on colliers and so continues almost to the very end: Mercutio, and even Juliet, quibble in death. Punning, of course, is not the only sort of verbal jugglery in the play, *e.g.* the overdone oxymoron in Romeo's first speech of any length.

In *Romeo and Juliet* Shakespeare makes full use of dramatic irony—the difference between the situation as known to the audience and as supposed by the characters of the play or by some of them. The basis of dramatic irony is ambiguity of meaning. A remark may have a surface meaning for the characters in the play but an added significance for the audience. The double meaning may be intended by the speaker or just casual. The secrecy of the marriage of Romeo and Juliet lends itself to dramatic irony. When Lady Capulet is denouncing Romeo, Juliet appears to agree with her, but her phrases are double-edged.

> Ay, madam, from the reach of these my hands:
> Would none but I might venge my cousin's death!

> Indeed, I never shall be satisfied
> With Romeo, till I behold him—dead—
> Is my poor heart so for a kinsman vex'd.

When Romeo has fallen in love with Juliet, Mercutio imagines that he is still moping for Rosaline.

> Ah, that same pale hard-hearted wench, that
>   Rosaline,
> Torments him so that he will sure run mad.

Similarly, Lady Capulet imagines that Juliet is upset owing to Tybalt's murder (III. iv. 11). The Nurse tells Juliet of a "bloody piteous corse", and Juliet, thinking that it must be Romeo's, exclaims, "And thou and Romeo press one heavy bier!" Little did she think when she spoke these words that they would be made true. In answer to Juliet's last words to him, "O, think'st thou we shall ever meet again?", Romeo says, "I doubt it not". So it was, but not in the sense in which he meant it (see also pp. 15-16). Lady Capulet plans her revenge on Romeo by "an unaccustom'd dram, that he shall soon keep Tybalt company", and so does it fall out, but not by her ordering.

In a good play the style naturally reflects the character of the person speaking, and even the same man in two different moods may speak in two different ways. Contrast the airy tone of Mercutio's famous "Queen Mab" speech (I. iv), light as a soap bubble, with the staid speeches of the Prince and Friar Laurence—or even Benvolio. Look at Capulet's long speech in Act I, Sc. ii, and contrast this with his jerky, disjointed speech when his temper is up (III. v), or when he is fussily hurrying about giving orders for the wedding feast (IV. iv).

There occur in *Romeo and Juliet* little circumstantial details (used sparingly, so as not to interfere with the main impression) which give clearer definition to the picture. "The grove of sycamore that westward rooteth from the city's side", the nightingale that nightly "sings on yon pomegranate-tree", the "*twenty* cunning cooks" to be hired for the feast, are three examples from the play, and the student will find others for himself.

The use Shakespeare makes of contrast in larger measure in the construction of his play has already been mentioned (see p. 13). It should also be noticed in the phrasing of single lines (antithesis), *e.g.* "More light and light; more dark and dark our woes!"

Nearly one-eighth of *Romeo and Juliet* is in prose. When prose is used in Shakespeare's plays it is for a definite purpose. Prose is invariably the language of comic characters and characters of lower social position. This was a literary convention at a time when literature was aristocratic and the chief characters in plays (as in life) were kings and nobles. Scenes in which the lower orders of society figure are a contrast; these people live on a lower plane of feeling than the main characters, and thereby emphasise the height of the feeling of the main characters, and the contrast in the medium of expression—prose instead of verse—is in perfect keeping.

In Act I, Sc. i the servants talk in prose and those of noble family in verse, and this distinction is kept throughout the play. Sometimes the reason for prose is a lower pitch of feeling without a lower social position in the speaker, for example the jocular talk of Benvolio, Mercutio and Romeo in Act II, Sc. iv. But when Benvolio and Mercutio have gone Romeo thinks of Juliet and tells the Nurse of the plans he has made to marry her in verse. In the following scene the Nurse (who probably speaks in verse anywhere only owing to her close association with Juliet) alternates between verse and prose according to the tone of her speech—whether it is concerned with the matter in hand or is just bantering prattle from nurse to child. Similarly in III. i the emotional pitch determines whether prose or verse shall be the medium. In the last Act the Apothecary and the Watch no doubt speak in verse because they are caught up in great events. Juliet always speaks in verse.

Formal communications (*e.g.* the list of people invited to Capulet's mask) are, of course, in prose.

THE ELIZABETHAN THEATRE AND ITS EFFECT ON PLAYS

At the time of Shakespeare there were probably not more than five public theatres in the land, all in London, and they were built according to the design of the inn-yards of the period, which had been found marvellously convenient places for the presentation of plays.

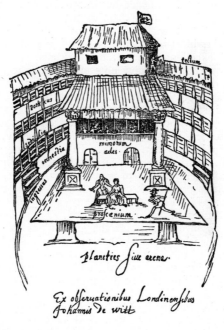

(Reproduced by kind permission of Messrs. Blackie & Sons, Ltd.)

The theatre was circular or octagonal in shape. The main part of the auditorium was the large round pit, open to the sky, in which the poorer people *stood* (the "groundlings"). Encircling this, round the walls, were three balconies, covered on top but not in front (like the "stands" on a football ground), and containing seats. The price of admission to the pit was one penny, equivalent to about one shilling and ninepence nowadays, and balcony seats ranged from twopence to half-a-crown, according to their position. When it was wet the performance was postponed until the next day.

The stage was large, jutting far into the pit, and was without scenery and any but the most meagre properties. Hence it made no difference that people stood at the side of the stage as well as in front. The scenery was created in the imagination of the audience by the words of the characters in the play: it was made part of the play, so as not to obtrude and destroy the illusion of reality (*e.g.* II. ii. 107-108, III. iii. 1-6). That is why Shakespeare's plays make such excellent sound radio broadcasts. As you listen in your arm-chair you have no scenery, but the scenery is in the words of the play and so is created in your mind.

The play went straight on without pauses. Lack of pauses and frequent changes of scene were immaterial when the stage was without scenery, consequently a succession of short scenes, as Act IV, Scenes ii, iii and iv, is quite common in Elizabethan drama. In a modern play with change of scenery the audience would become impatient at the constant delays. There is good reason to believe that Shakespeare's plays took considerably less time than they do to-day. The Prologue to *Romeo and Juliet* refers to "the two hours' traffic of our stage".

In the absence of curtains the end of a scene was frequently shown by rhyming lines, as at the end of the first three scenes of the play. A similar use is at the end of a long account in a scene, as at the end of Benvolio's relation of "the unlucky manage of this fatal brawl" to the Prince in Act III, Sc. i.

Just as the scenery had to be *put into* the play, so had entrances and exits to be arranged as *part of the play*. To-day an actor can get into position before the rise of the curtain, but on the open stage it would seem artificial if he walked on, and then started his part, or finished the scene and then walked off. Such endings as these in the same three scenes of the first Act clear the stage and at the same time fit in perfectly naturally with the play— "Farewell", "I'll go along", "We follow thee. Juliet, the county stays". It follows that dead bodies always had to be carried off the stage, as at the end of Act III, Sc. i—

"Bear hence this body". In Mercutio's case he is helped off the stage before he dies.

It was not unknown for the stage floor to be equipped with a trap-door for the sudden appearance and disappearance of ghosts and spirits.

At the back of the stage was a recess "within", and this was curtained and could be shut off when desired. The recess may have served for Friar Laurence's cell and for the Capulet tomb. In Act IV, Sc. v we are told that the Nurse "undraws the curtains".

Above the recess was a balcony, which served for an upper room, castle walls and suchlike scenes. This, too, could be curtained off. People were fond of balcony scenes, particularly when there was an escape from the balcony—an upper room, for example—to the main stage —representing the ground below. Much use is made of the balcony in *Romeo and Juliet*. At the beginning of Act II, Sc. i Romeo climbs a wall and drops down again. In the next scene "Juliet appears *above* at a window" and later speaks to Romeo on the main stage below, and in Act III, Sc. v Romeo escapes from the balcony down the "cords".

Young men of the day who wished to attract public notice actually hired stools round the stage itself. It was a source of continual annoyance to playwrights that actors "gagged" in order to please these aristocratic playgoers.

No women were allowed to act by law. Consequently women's parts had to be taken by boys with unbroken voices. Imagine a boy's rendering of Lady Macbeth or Cleopatra, or even Juliet, who was, indeed, only thirteen herself (see p. 11). The ban on actresses accounts for the few women's parts in plays of the period, though some were always introduced for the sake of variety. In *Romeo and Juliet* there are but four, and this is more than usual in Shakespeare's plays. It also accounts for the large number of plays where a woman disguises herself as a page boy. It made it much easier for the producer; further, the audience was intrigued by a situation in which a character was pretending to be what he really was! In *The Merchant of Venice* every one of the women disguises herself as a man.

Plays were not acted in period costume. Thus all Shakespeare's plays were first acted in "modern dress". Although there was no scenery, managers spared no expense on the most lavish of costumes.

On days when the theatre was open a flag was flown from the turret, and when the play was about to begin a trumpet was sounded.

One must not imagine that it was difficult for Shakespeare to write plays for such a theatre. It would have been difficult for him to write for any other than the one he was used to. What we have never known we never miss.

THE TEXT OF SHAKESPEARE'S PLAYS

FEW readers of Shakespeare realise the difficulties scholars have had to overcome in order to establish accurate texts of the plays. The First Folio (see pp. 6-7) contained thirty-six plays. Other collected editions or Folios were published in the seventeenth century, the Third and Fourth Folios containing seven additional plays, none of which, with the exception of *Pericles*, is now thought to be by Shakespeare. Sixteen of the plays had already been published separately as Quartos before 1623, and in the case of some plays, for example, *Hamlet*, more than one Quarto edition exists. Some of these Quartos are almost word for word the same as the texts in the First Folio and were possibly set up from Shakespeare's own manuscript or at least from accurate theatre copies; but others are shortened, inferior versions, possibly "pirated" editions published by some unauthorised person who had access to theatre copies or parts of them, or who had taken down the plays in shorthand while they were being performed. It is thought that the texts of the First Folio were set up from the good Quartos and from good theatre copies. But these texts must all be compared, printers' mistakes and other interference traced, before a reliable text can be arrived at. The first editor to attempt the problem of the text was Nicholas Rowe (1674-1718), to whom we also owe the division of most of the plays into acts and scenes, place references at the heads of the scenes, indications of entrances and exits, and lists of dramatis personæ, which are absent from many of the texts in the Quarto and Folio editions. There is no division of any kind between scenes in the earliest texts of *Romeo and Juliet*; the play ran swiftly on, and divisions were unnecessary upon a stage with the barest of scenery. Rowe's divisions in this play can be used only for convenience in reference (like the division of the books of the Bible into chapter and verse) and occasionally he makes an obvious mistake (see note on "He . . . wound", p. 70).

NOTES

Prologue

PROLOGUE. The Prologue is in the form of a regular Shakespearean sonnet—a poem of 14 lines (iambic pentameters) rhyming *a b a b, c d c d, e f, e f, g g*, with a break in the thought after the 8th line. The first 8 lines (octave) here outline the story and the last 6 (sestet) turn to it in the play. A prologue (or chorus) is unusual in Shakespeare's plays.

Chorus. The speaker of the Prologue. The name is taken from Greek drama (where a Chorus of singers commonly played a part as interpreters of the play) but in Elizabethan plays it is a single actor.

alike, equal.

Verona. A city of Northern Italy, some 70 miles almost due west of Venice.

grudge, hatred—a stronger word than now.

mutiny, disorder, tumult—between anyone, not just in the armed forces.

Where, in which.

civil blood makes civil hands unclean, the blood of the citizens in civil war makes the hands of a civilised (well-mannered) people unclean. (Metonymy and synecdoche.)

fatal, *i.e.* destined to produce issue fated for misfortune.

star-cross'd, *i.e.* their fortunes were marred by the influence of the stars. That men's natures and fortunes were influenced by the star under which they were born was a widespread superstition of Elizabethan times.

Whose . . . strife, the cessation of whose unfortunate pitiful struggles makes an end to their parents' strife. "Overthrows" is a noun, not a verb.

death-mark'd, destined (marked out) for death.

but, except for.

the two . . . stage. See p. 46.

miss, fail, be missing, perhaps an implied metaphor, *i.e.* miss the mark.

ACT I. SCENE I VERONA A PUBLIC PLACE

There is an ancient feud between the houses of Capulet and Montague in Verona.

Two retainers of the house of Capulet stir up a street brawl with two of their opposite numbers in the house of Montague, and Benvolio, nephew to Montague, is unable to restore the peace, and is set on by Tybalt, nephew to Lady Capulet, who refuses to listen to talk of peace ("I hate the word"). Others join in from both sides, then Citizens, who are sick to death of these constant breaches of the peace—"Down with the Capulets! down with the Montagues!" Lord and Lady Capulet and Lord and Lady Montague appear, closely followed by the Prince, who quells the disturbance and says that upon the next brawl between them Capulet and Montague shall answer for it with their lives. They are ordered to appear before him to hear his "further pleasure in this case". People withdraw and peace is restored.

Lady Montague wonders what has become of her son Romeo, and is told by Benvolio that he has been keeping his own company lately. Montague cannot understand why Romeo is "so secret and so close", and Benvolio undertakes to try to find out. He discovers that Romeo is in love but that his love is unrequited. He cannot find out who the lady is, however. Romeo talks of his love in conventional, superficial language, making use of many verbal quibbles.

The play gets under way very quickly. Within five minutes of the start there is mob uproar. By contrast the second half of the scene passes in quiet talk about an absent youngster who is passing his time in brooding concealment and who before the end is found to be suffering from the pains of unrequited love.

carry coals, *i.e.* put up with insults—be treated as the lowest servants.

colliers. In Shakespeare's time the word was used as a term of abuse. A collier was a coal carrier (not a miner).

an we be in choler, if we are angry, if our blood is up.

draw, *i.e.* draw our swords.

collar, *i.e* halter. Notice the punning on "collier", "choler" and "collar", and on the two senses of "draw". This sort of word-play is characteristic of the play throughout (see p. 42).

moved, roused to anger, stirred.

But . . . moved, *i.e.* it takes a lot to rouse you.

A dog, *i.e.* any low-down fellow.

move me to stand, incite me to take up my stand and fight.

take the wall, get the better of. In those days of filthy pavements and gutters full of refuse, if two people met on the pavement the stronger man took the best position, *i.e.* near the wall, away from the gutter (in the middle of the street).

goes to the wall, *i.e.* the other extreme, is *pushed against* the wall.

men, *i.e.* servants.

between . . . men, *i.e.* we will not bring the women into it.

'Tis all one, *i.e.* 'tis all the same, it makes no difference to me.

maidenheads, maidenhood.

in sense. Punning on "sense" meaning "feeling" (as in the word "sensuous").

if thou hadst, *i.e.* if thou hadst been.

poor John, hake or cod dried and salted, hence poor fare.

comes. Colloquial.

quarrel, I will back thee, quarrel, and I will back you up, support you. See note on "thou's", p. 59.

me, *i.e.* what I shall do.

marry. An oath—*lit.* "by the Virgin Mary", but in effect no stronger than "indeed".

take the law of, have the law on.

list, please.

bite my thumb. An insulting gesture in Shakespeare's time.

bear, put up with.

for you, *i.e.* ready to fight you.

Well, sir. Sampson cannot understand what Abraham means by his non-committal reply. He could mean that there was no better master than his own or that there was no better master than Sampson's.

one of my master's kinsmen. Tybalt; evidently he does not see Benvolio.

swashing blow, *i.e.* knock-out blow, *lit.* a blow that comes down with a swishing noise.

heartless hinds, cowardly serving-men. The implication is that it is beneath Benvolio's rank to fight with such low fellows, in Tybalt he would have an opponent worthy of his steel.

thy death, *i.e.* my sword (which will cause it).

manage, use.

Have at thee, there's for you.

Clubs. The cry of the London apprentices to call their fellows, sometimes to come with their clubs to keep the peace, as often as not to create a disturbance.

bills, pikes.

partisans. Similar to "bills". They looked like bayonets on long wooden poles.

gown, *i.e.* dressing-gown.

long sword, *i.e.* sword for action, not one to be worn merely for fashion's sake.

A crutch, *i.e.* at your time of life a crutch would be of more use than a sword.

spite, despite, defiance.

Hold me not. Spoken to his wife.

Profaners . . . steel, *i.e.* you profane your weapons by staining them with the blood of your neighbours.

mistemper'd, temper'd for a bad use.

sentence, judgment.

moved. See note p. 51.

airy, *i.e.* ill-considered.

ancient, old.

Cast by, throw aside.

beseeming ornaments, weapons befitting them (*i.e.* walking-sticks).

To, in order to.

Canker'd, rusted up.

forfeit of, penalty for breaking.

For this time, on this occasion, for now.

our further pleasure, what also we wish to do. The "our" is the royal plural, used throughout the speech.

Free-town. In Brooke's poem (see p. 8) the name of Capulet's castle ("Villa Franca" in the original Italian story).

new abroach, starting anew—metaphor from broaching a cask.

by, *i.e.* near by.

close, *i.e.* in the thick of a fight.

in the instant, at that moment, at the same time.

prepared, *i.e.* drawn.

Who. Antecedent "the winds".

nothing hurt withal, not at all hurt thereby.

hiss'd him in scorn. Refers to the swish of his sword through the air.

more and more, *i.e.* more and more people.

part and part, one side or the other.

parted either part, separated both sides.

forth, forth from.

sycamore. Traditionally associated with disappointed lovers.

westward . . . side, grows on the west side of the city. See p. 44.

made, *i.e.* made my way.

ware, aware.

affections, feelings, desires.

most might not be found, fewest people might be found.

humour, inclination. *Cf.* the title of Ben Jonson's play *Every Man in his Humour* (*i.e.* according to his mood, temperament or disposition).

who, him who.

all so soon as, as soon as ever.

Aurora. Goddess of the dawn in classical mythology.

heavy, *i.e.* heavy at heart. An antithesis with "light" (in another sense).

pens, locks up (as an animal is penned).

portentous, ominous, threatening.

importuned, made a continual effort to question him.

his own affections' counsellor, *i.e.* keeping his own counsel about his feelings (not sharing his troubles so that anyone else may give "his own affections" counsel).

true, *i.e.* true to himself.

sounding, revelation—the same meaning as "discovery". A metaphor from sounding the depth of water in navigation.

envious, malignant.

know, *i.e.* know what the trouble is.

Enter **Romeo.** Dramatically it is much more effective to "lead up'' to Romeo like this, in the conversation of minor characters, than to bring him on the stage at the outset. This method has the advantage of creating suspense, and when the main character appears he appears in response to a longing of the audience to see him. Our imagination has been worked upon by the talk of Benvolio, Montague and his Lady, so that when Romeo appears he already has our interest. From a practical point of view it also means that the first speeches of the main character are not disturbed by the entry of latecomers: by the time he speaks the audience has settled down.

so please you, so may it please you, the common phraseology of a polite request in Elizabethan times.

grievance, cause of grief or suffering.

be much denied, *i.e.* he will have to refuse me many times, for I will keep on at him—I will "importune" him.

happy, fortunate.

shrift, confession.

morrow, morning.

cousin. The two were actually cousins, although the term in Elizabethan use was a common friendly greeting.

new, just (newly).

makes, *i.e.* would make.

where, with whom.

view, appearance. When Romeo uses the word he means "sight of others".

proof, experience, reality.

still, always—the usual meaning in Elizabethan English.

his will, *i.e.* make people fall in love. Cupid, the god of love, was represented as blind in classical mythology.

fray. Romeo sees signs of the recent brawl.

more with love. Perhaps because Rosaline belonged to the Capulet family (as we see from the list of invited guests, Sc. ii), or he may mean that there is more in his heart to do with love.

loving hate. This and the following pairings of opposites are examples of the figure of speech known as oxymoron.

create, created.

well-seeming, apparently beautiful.

Still-waking, keeping awake all the time. See note on "still", above.

no love, *i.e.* no really satisfying love.

coz. A contraction of "cousin", see note above.

transgression. In making lovers suffer so.

propagate, increase.

thine, *i.e.* thy griefs.

love, *i.e.* love of me.

vex'd, disturbed—a stronger word than now.

A choking . . . sweet, a substance bitter enough to choke (anyone) and sweet enough to preserve (something).

Soft! A common exclamation of Shakespeare's time, equivalent to "Wait a minute!".

along, *i.e.* with you.

An if. Both words mean the same, so that one is redundant. *Cf.* note on "an we be in choler", p. 51.

some other where, somewhere else.

sadness, seriousness (a common meaning in Shakespeare).

groan. Romeo purposely misunderstands "sadness", as if used in its modern sense—"Shall I groan in sadness?"

sadly, seriously. Benvolio uses the word with the same meaning as he did before.

sadness. Used first with the meaning Benvolio had given it, and then with both meanings—seriousness and sadness.

ill urged, unkindly or wrongly pressed home.

aim'd so near, guessed as much. (Benvolio wants to know *which* woman Romeo loves.)

mark-man. Now "marksman".

fair mark, clear target. Benvolio plays on the word "fair" in a different sense, as Romeo does with Benvolio's "hit", using it in the sense of "guess". There are many metaphors from archery in Shakespeare and in Elizabethan literature generally.

Cupid. Roman god of love. Those pierced by his golden arrows were smitten by love. *Cf.* note on "his will", p. 54.

Dian's wit, the good sense of Diana, Roman goddess of chastity.

proof, tested armour.

From, by.

stay, endure, abide, matching "bide" in the next line.

the siege. The military metaphor is continued.

assailing, *i.e.* with looks of love.

her store, *i.e.* her store of wealth (which consists in her beauty). She will leave no beauty behind her in her offspring. This is a continual thought in Shakespeare's sonnets.

waste, *i.e.* of beauty (in the children who will·never be born).

starved, killed (not necessarily by lack of food).

bliss, *i.e.* in heaven.

live dead. So do we talk of a "living death" (Oxymoron). See note on "loving hate", p. 54.

ruled, advised.

how . . . think, *i.e.* he can think of nothing else.

'Tis . . . more, it would be the way to make me more conscious of her beauty, which is exquisite.

passing, surpassingly.

What doth her beauty serve, what is the use of her beauty?

note, memorandum.

pass'd, surpassed (in the same sense as "passing", above).

I'll pay that doctrine, *i.e.* I will pay you back in your own coin and show you that you cannot teach *me* to forget (to try to make *you* forget). Romeo says that Benvolio cannot teach him to forget, and in effect Benvolio says that he will have a good try.

ACT I. SCENE II *The Same A Street.*

The Count Paris asks Capulet for the hand of his daughter, but is refused on account of her youth (thirteen years). He will not think of her marriage for another two years, and even then he will not impose his choice upon her. If Paris can "get her heart" he will readily consent. Paris is invited to "an old accustom'd feast" at his house that night.

Capulet then gives a servant a list of guests to be sought out and invited. The servant cannot read, however, and when he falls in with Romeo and Benvolio asks them to read out the names, before he goes giving them a casual invitation too, if they "be not of the house of Montagues". From the list they learn that Rosaline, Romeo's beloved, is to be one of the guests, and Benvolio, continuing his cure of Romeo's love-sickness, persuades him to go to the supper and see how many ladies more beautiful than Rosaline there are amongst "the admired beauties of Verona".

This scene happens in the late afternoon of the same day as the previous scene. (Montague has already been "bound"—see i. 87.)

In Scene i we met the hero; in Scene ii our interest is aroused in the heroine (see note on *"Enter* Romeo", p. 53) and we learn something of the background of her life.

bound, *i.e.* to keep the peace.

penalty alike, the same penalty.

reckoning. In view of Capulet's speech and the following line in Paris's speech, it would seem that Paris refers to the reckoning of their years, *i.e.* experience of life, not to their reputation in general.

odds, enmity.

But saying o'er, only saying over again.

a stranger, *i.e.* she has not yet "come out".

wither in their pride, *i.e.* let their beautiful flowers wither. So do we talk of "the pride of summer".

marr'd. made. A thoroughly Shakespearean antithesis. There is an undoubted reference to the proverb, "Soon married, soon marred".

The earth . . . hopes, *i.e.* all my (other) children are dead and buried.

earth, *i.e.* body, offspring. Capulet *may* mean that his daughter is the heiress of his land, but it seems not so likely, as in this speech Capulet's mind is not on material things.

My will . . . part, my permission follows on (is but a part of) her choice.

An, if. See note on "an we be in choler", p. 51, and "an if", p. 55.

scope, range.

according, agreeing.

accustom'd, established by custom.

Earth-treading stars, *i.e.* beautiful ladies.

limping, *i.e.* old and worn out.

Inherit, have, enjoy, take part in.

Which . . . none. This is differently punctuated in different editions, giving two different meanings. (1) When you have seen more of her whose merit is most (the antecedent of "which"), many—including my daughter—may be in the company, but none may be reckoned with her. (2) When you have seen many ladies, my daughter being one, she may be one of the company, but not one for whom you have any esteem. (1) has a comma at "of", and (2) at "many". The first seems more in character, in view of Capulet's words about what his daughter means to him, but if the second be accepted it could be said that he wants to save his daughter from an unhappy marriage, and make sure that Paris's mind is made up and that his affection is not a passing fancy.

sirrah. A familiar (or contemptuous) form of "sir", generally used when speaking to inferiors.

trudge, walk—with no sense of heavy, laborious steps as in modern English.

on their pleasure stay, await their pleasure. *Cf.* note on "stay", p. 55.

the shoemaker . . . nets. The servant (or clown) mixes up the terms of equipment that the various tradesmen use. "Yard" = yard-measure.

writ, written.

must, must go.

the learned, *i.e.* someone who can read.

In good time. Said as he sees Benvolio and Romeo coming "in good time".

Tut. An expression of impatience. Benvolio is still "paying that doctrine" (see his last speech in Sc. i). For the style of this speech, like the sestet of a Shakespearean sonnet, see note on "PROLOGUE", p. 50.

one fire burns out another's burning, *i.e.* a greater fire soon burns up the material of a lesser, or Benvolio may be referring to the country superstition that the sun puts out a fire in a grate. Really, of course, it is only that the fire cannot be seen.

another's anguish, *i.e.* the anguish of another pain.

holp, helped.

backward, in the opposite direction.

cures with another's anguish. On the parallel of the "pain" this would mean "is cured when another (grief) brings a depressing effect".

Your plantain-leaf, a dock-leaf. Romeo means that a dock-leaf is useful for minor ills—to stop bleeding from a scratch, for instance—but *his* ailment needs a more desperate remedy. "Your" has no significance; it is used as an indefinite article for some common thing with which both people are familiar.

your broken shin, *i.e.* shin of which the skin has been broken. "Your" is used in the same way as above.

more, *i.e.* more heavily. Romeo's restraints come from himself, however.

God-den, good evening, a contraction of the fuller form used by the servant—in full, "God give you a good even". In Elizabethan times this greeting was given any time after noon.

rest you merry! A colloquial term of farewell, comparable to our "All the best!" "Rest" = remain.

County. Another form of "Count", not infrequently used by Shakespeare.

Rosaline. The first time Romeo's lady-love is named.

should they, are they to.

Up. As we say, "To our place".

that, *i.e.* who your master is.

crush a cup. A common colloquial expression in Elizabethan English, comparable to "crack a bottle".

ancient, one which has been held annually for a long time, "accustom'd" (see note p. 57).

unattainted, impartial.

show, point out to you.

devout religion. Implying that he worships Rosaline.

these, *i.e.* these eyes of mine ("drown'd" in tears).

match, equal.

you saw her, *i.e.* she appeared to you.

either eye, *i.e.* in each of your eyes.

scales, pair of scales, hence thought of as singular. The scales are Romeo's eyes, thus "crystal".

lady's love, love for your lady. To interpret "the slight love of your lady for you" shifts the emphasis and is unlikely.

shining, *i.e.* as a star, see l. 25.

scant show well, scarcely appear attractive.

along. See note p. 54.

splendour of mine own, the splendid beauty of my own beloved.

ACT I. SCENE III *Room in Capulet's House*

On the evening of the same day Lady Capulet comes to tell Juliet what an eligible young man Paris is, and Juliet says that she will do her best to love him. They leave quickly when a servant comes in announcing that they are waited for at the supper table.

This scene shows us Juliet unaffected by love (but as an obedient daughter willing to consider her mother's choice) before she meets Romeo, just as the previous scenes have shown us Romeo in love with someone else before he meets Juliet.

maidenhead. See note p. 52.

lady-bird. A term of endearment, similar to "lamb". (The lady-bird is a small and beautiful insect.)

God forbid! *i.e.* that anything should have happened to her.

Juliet. The first time that she is named.

How now! *i.e.* what's the matter now?

Your mother. Juliet is the only important Shakespearean heroine with a mother alive at the time of the play. See p. 26.

give leave. A polite way of saying, "Take your leave".

remember'd me. The "me" can be ignored. Actually it is a reflexive use, *lit.* "reminded myself".

thou's, thou shalt. The Elizabethan use of "thou" and "you" is clearly shown in this conversation. "Thou" was a sign of familiarity (used by a master or mistress to servants and between close friends), "you" was a formal address used by servant to master. Lady Capulet addresses the nurse as "thou", whereas the nurse addresses her as "you". But Juliet, her young charge, with whom she was on very close terms, she addresses as "thou" ("Thou wast the prettiest babe"). Lady Capulet addresses Juliet as "you". When the servant comes in at the end of the scene he addresses Lady Capulet as "you", and Lady Capulet replies, "We follow *thee*". Compare also the conversation between Sampson and Gregory in the first scene; also that between Tybalt and Benvolio which follows (where Tybalt uses the second person contemptuously, as towards an inferior) and that between Montague and Benvolio after Romeo's entrance (though previously Montague had addressed his nephew as "you"). The student will readily find other examples.

since the earthquake. There was an earthquake in England in 1580 and a bad one in Verona in 1570, but no reference to any particular earthquake need be inferred. Some have taken the reference to be to the 1580 earthquake and have deduced therefrom that the date of the writing of the play was 1591, but the garrulous old Nurse is not one whose memory is to be trusted, though it is true that such people have a knack of remembering the time and circumstances of what has affected themselves.

wormwood. A plant with a bitter juice to make the child stop drinking (foster-) mother's milk.

Mantua. The actual situation matters little, especially in this context, but for students who prefer to have everything lined up exactly for their examination the town is just over 25 miles S.S.W. of Verona.

brain, *i.e.* memory.

fool. A term of endearment—darling or innocent.

tetchy, peevish.

'Shake' quoth the dove house, the dove-house began shaking— a colloquial use of "quoth" still occasionally found in small rural communities of Warwickshire.

'twas, there was.

trudge, walk away. See note p. 57. There was no need to send her away, because she then knew that her duties were finished.

trow, believe.

then she could stand alone. If Juliet was not weaned and could not stand up by herself until she was two or three years old, she was a very backward child.

rood, cross (of Christ).

broke, *i.e.* broke the skin of. See note on "your broken shin", p. 57.

halidom, *lit.* holy thing—the expression was a current oath.

stinted, stopped.

parlous, perilous.

to, for.

live . . . once, only live to see you married.

Marry. Used here with the same meaning as in note p. 52.

disposition, inclination.

were not I thine only nurse. But since she is, to say so would be to praise herself. The nurse says it by saying that she will not say it, as ignorant people often do.

of esteem, well-esteemed.

by my count, *i.e.* if I remember rightly.

of wax, *i.e.* as handsome as if he had been modelled in wax—finer than men usually are.

married, *i.e.* symmetrical, well-balanced.

one another lends content, one sets off another to advantage. "One" is the subject of "lends", and is not to be taken with "another", the indirect object. It is not likely that "content" means "subject-matter" (contents), though it may be a secondary association in a passage full of word-play.

margent, margin, edge; the place for comments in old books (*e.g.* old Bibles). The general sense is that what you cannot find written in his face you will find out in his eyes.

unbound, *i.e.* not attached to anyone (playing on the word in two senses, the other being the metaphor from a book).

cover, the binding (bonds) of marriage.

fair without . . . hide, *i.e.* for the beautiful sea to contain beautiful fish. "Without" and "within" are nouns. There may be an implication that fish are in the sea to be caught.

That in . . . story, *i.e.* is beautiful to look at on the outside as well as having a beautiful story within. The book "shares the glory" of "golden clasps" on the outside and a "golden story" within. Old books with clasps to lock them can be seen in museums: in those (Shakespeare's) days books were valuable things. There is, of course, a pun on the clasps of a lover. The application is that Paris has a fair appearance "outside" and a good character "within".

making yourself no less, at the same time not lessening your own possessions (or importance).

like of, like, approve of.

look, try, expect.

looking liking move, what I see makes me like him. "Looking" is the subject of "move", "liking" the object.

But no . . . fly, *i.e.* I will go no farther than you approve. "Endart" = sink into the target (like a dart or an arrow).

cursed, *i.e.* for her absence.

extremity, a muddle.

wait, *i.e.* upon the guests.

straight, at once, immediately.

stays, is waiting. See note on "on their pleasure stay", p. 57.

ACT I. SCENE IV ~Same A Street.~

The Montague team is in the street on its way to Capulet's mask (to take place after the supper to which Juliet and her mother were going at the end of Scene iii). Romeo does not feel in the mood for dancing, and, in fact, senses a premonition of some bitter consequence proceeding from "this night's revels".

The scene does nothing to advance the plot; it does, however, contribute to an atmosphere of foreboding at the end. Much of it is taken up by Mercutio's light, fanciful chatter, which is a contrast to Romeo's heavy presentiments.

Maskers. Men masked for a masquerade—a masked ball, not a masque, the elaborate entertainment which was coming into fashion among the nobility at the end of Shakespeare's career.

Torch-bearers. A torchlight procession regularly preceded a mask.

this speech, *i.e.* speech of apology (for coming to the ball without a formal invitation) as the next line shows.

on, go on.

The date is out, it is no longer the fashion.

Cupid. A guest disguised as Cupid (see note p. 55) as a spokesman to make their speech of apology.

hoodwink'd, blindfolded. See note on "his will", p. 54.

Tartar's painted bow of lath, *i.e.* an imitation (painted and of lath) of a Tartar bow (such as Cupid is represented with, not an English long-bow). "Tartar's" simply means "Easterner's" in a general sense, not specifically native to Tartary.

crow-keeper, scare-crow.

Nor no. In Elizabethan English a double negative intensifies the idea instead of logically cancelling it.

without-book, impromptu, or perhaps from memory.

measure . . . will, judge us how they please.

measure them a measure, dance a measure (a slow and stately dance) —punning on the word as used in the previous note.

Give me a torch, *i.e.* I do not want to dance, so I will be one of the torch-bearers.

ambling. A contemptuous word for dancing.

heavy. light. Romeo is rather fond of this punning antithesis. In I. i, he spoke of "heavy lightness", and Montague too said, "Away from light steals home my heavy son" (I. i). "Heavy" = heavy of heart.

So, which so.

bound, jump, leap upwards.

enpierced with his shaft. See note on "Cupid", p. 55.

pitch. A metaphor from falconry. The "pitch" was the technical word for the height to which a falcon soared before swooping on her prey.

to sink in it, should you, if you sank into love, you would.

Prick love for pricking, *i.e.* give love back as good (or as bad) as it gives you, or, in modern metaphor, pay it back in its own coin.

case, mask.

A visor for a visor! *i.e.* fancy putting a mask on *my* face, which is funny enough to be a mask by itself.

curious, careful, prying.

quote, note.

Here . . . me. Mercutio means that he cares not what people think of him, he does not want anyone to be embarrassed for him: if anyone blushes for him, it shall be himself.   "Beetle brows" = overhanging (eye)brows.

betake him to his legs, *i.e.* in dancing.   We shall then, he infers, be lost in the crowd and less likely to be noticed.

rushes. This one word gives us a wealth of Elizabethan local colour. See p. 17.

proverb'd with a grandsire phrase, supported by an old man's proverb (that the candle-holder, or looker-on, sees most of the game).

The game . . . done, this is the best part of the proceedings, so I am giving up before worse comes.   Another proverb, recommending people to give up while things are at their best, before the good impression is lost.

dun's the mouse. A slang Elizabethan phrase meaning "Keep quiet", hence "The constable's own word".

If . . . mire. "Dun is in the mire" is an old country game.   Dun was a log standing for a cart horse in the mire.   In moving the log there was much fun and merriment, such as pushing one another down and trying to make the log fall on one another's toes.

sir-reverence, filth, dung (a special form of "mire").   "Sir-reverence" came to mean this because the word prefaced mention of unpleasant things (a corruption of "save your reverence", *i.e.* excuse my mentioning it).   Used like this before mention of dung it came in time to replace the word itself.

we burn daylight, *i.e.* we are wasting time (from the burning of candles in daylight), as Mercutio explains.

light, we light.

good, proper.

in that, *i.e.* in our "good meaning".

five wits, *i.e.* being clever in playing with words.

mask. See note on "Maskers", p. 61.

wit, good sense.

to-night, last night.

lie, *i.e.* their dreams do not come true.

Queen Mab. Spoken of here as the Queen of the Fairies.   Mab was chief of the Irish fairies, and "Mab" in Welsh means "child" or "baby", so possibly Shakespeare may have met the name in a story from Welsh or Irish folk-lore.

fairies' midwife, *i.e.* delivering dreams that fill men's brains.

agate-stone, *i.e.* the figure cut on the stone in a ring, *e.g.* a seal-ring, in other words something very small.

atomies, atoms, very small creatures.

long spinners' legs, daddy-long-legs.

cover, *i.e.* hood of the "waggon".

traces, joining the horse to the "waggon".

collars, *i.e.* of the horses.

worm, parasite.

Prick'd, *i.e.* with a needle.

lazy. Because laziness was thought to induce such growths.

joiner, carpenter.

old grub. The grub bores his way through nuts, as the squirrel cracks them.

state, pomp and ceremony.

tainted. Presumably because their breaths are not naturally sweet and they use flavoured sweetmeats to smother the foulness.

smelling out a suit, *i.e.* seeking to obtain one from a monarch.

tithe-pig, *i.e.* a pig given in payment of tithe (*lit.* a tax of a tenth, paid to the Church—the "parson").

breaches, gaps made (by the attackers) in fortifications.

ambuscadoes, ambushes.

Spanish blades. Perhaps the swords of Spanish soldiers—the chief enemy of the English in those days, or perhaps the meaning is finely-tempered swords.

five-fathom deep, *i.e.* never-ending.

anon, straight away, immediately, at once (*lit.* in one).

Drums. The signal for battle.

swears a prayer or two, *i.e.* swearing is so natural to him that he cannot pray without swearing.

bakes, clots.

elf-locks. When dirty hair became clotted together it was superstitiously put down to elves, hence "elf-locks". It happened only to filthy hair, hence "foul sluttish hairs".

untangled. Obviously "entangled".

learns, teaches.

fantasy, fancy.

woos . . . north, *i.e.* blows warmly on the northern wastes.

This wind, you talk of. Probably with the implication that Mercutio is a windbag.

from ourselves, away from our purpose.

yet hanging in the stars. See note on "star-cross'd", p. 50.

date, time of action.

expire, end, cause the expiry of.

lusty gentlemen. Corresponding to "my fine fellows".

Strike, drum. Spoken to the drummer-boy, a sign that they shall march on.

Act I. Scene v

Romeo and his companions are welcomed by old Capulet to his mask, and Tybalt, who would make trouble out of their presence, is held sternly in check by Capulet, and he leaves in a huff.

Romeo and Juliet fall suddenly and passionately in love. Juliet learns who Romeo is and after the mask is over—like Romeo before it began—feels a similar presentiment of evil.

Scenes ii and iv (on Romeo's side) and iii (on Juliet's) have led to the mask. Here the two strands meet, and hero and heroine are brought face to face.

Notice the difference between the real language of love at the end of this scene and Juliet's detached talk about Paris in Scene iii. She spoke with her mother about Paris, the conventional suitor, openly and without special interest; she cannot share with her mother the real feelings of her heart for Romeo—and it is not *only* because he is a Montague. This is closely parallel with the difference between Romeo's affected love-language about Rosaline and his silence (to his friends) when he *really* falls in love with Juliet.

The actual meeting of Romeo and Juliet is kept back. We know that it will come in this scene, but we are held in suspense while we listen to servants' chatter, and then again, after Romeo has seen (but not met) Juliet, by the talk between Tybalt and old Capulet. This dramatic delay all the more sharpens our desire to see what happens when they meet; we feel that we *must* know, we cannot wait any longer.

The trouble in the air which Romeo and Juliet both sense seems to lie not very far away—in Tybalt's rapier.

Note that Rosaline was invited to the mask, but that she is not mentioned at all. If she accepted the invitation, Romeo had no eyes for her.

The chatter of the servants about their business gives the impression of the passing of time between the maskers' setting off for the dance at the end of the previous scene and their arrival early in this one. No time-analysis can give a sense of the flight of time so well as the actual passing of other scenes before our eyes.

take away, clear away.

trencher, wooden plate, *lit.* one to cut food upon (Fr. "trencher"). In Warwickshire a bread board is still called a "trencher".

When . . . hands, *i.e.* when only one or two men do their duty.

foul. Punning on "shameful" and "dirty" (from the unwashed hands).

joint-stools, folding stools (not all in one piece).

court-cupboard, movable side-board, on which the food was placed.

plate, silver-plate.

thou. See note on "thou's", p. 59.

marchpane. Our nearest equivalent is almond cake. The modern form of the word is "marzipan".

great chamber, *i.e.* dining-hall.

Cheerly, heartily, with a good will.

the longer liver to take all. A proverb, meaning that he who lives longest will get the most.

the **Guests** *and* **Maskers.** Romeo and his friends.

bout. Metaphor for a dance.

deny, refuse. If they do refuse, after what has been said, it will be assumed that they have corns.

makes dainty, comes shyly.

come near ye, touched you on the raw—where it hurts.

A hall, *i.e.* clear the room.

knaves, boys, servants (without the deprecatory modern sense).

turn the tables up, *i.e* take them off their trestles, lay them flat against the wall.

quench the fire. Shakespeare here forgets that the play is supposed to happen in July (I. ii. 16), and is thinking of Brooke's poem, the events of which take place at Christmas-time. Act III, Sc. i happens on a hot day.

By 'r lady, by our Lady, *i.e.* the Virgin Mary.

nuptial, marriage.

pentecost, Whitsuntide.

his son is elder, his (Lucentio's) son is older.

Will you tell me. Spoken with the sense of disbelief in which we say, "Are you going to tell me . . . ?"

ward, minor, under somebody's guardianship.

enrich the hand, *i.e.* by dancing with him—he holds her hand.

Ethiope, negro—as used by Shakespeare (here and elsewhere), not Ethiopian in its narrower sense.

use, everyday wear.

fellows, *i.e.* fellow-dancers.

measure. See note on "measure them a measure", p. 61.

place of stand. Notice that in those days between dances dancers stood up, as, indeed, people did in Church, at parish meetings, etc.

rude, common.

it, *i.e.* his previous love.

sight. He appeals to his sight to forswear his previous love, on account of what follows in the next line.

should, *i.e.* must.

boy. Spoken to a servant (not necessarily of boy's years). See note on "knaves", p. 65, and "men", p. 52.

antic face, *i.e.* grinning mask.

fleer and scorn. Referring to his mask.

solemnity, ceremonial festival. The word was applied to any festival traditionally observed in a due form, not necessarily solemn in our sense. In IV. v. 60, it is applied to a wedding, and the meaning is clearly shown when the wedding music is to be changed to funeral music—"Our solemn hymns to sullen dirges change" (IV. v. 87).

stock, *i.e.* family stock, lineage.

Content thee, keep your temper. "Thee" is reflexive.

bears him, carries himself.

portly, dignified, honourable, of good carriage or bearing.

brags, speaks, with the implication that she is glad to do so.

well-govern'd, well-mannered.

disparagement, discourtesy.

patient, calm. Capulet does *not* mean, "Wait patiently for another opportunity".

presence, appearance, looks.

ill-beseeming semblance, ill-looking appearance.

goodman boy, my fine fellow—with the implication in "boy" that he is only an underling after all (see note above).

go to, stop it, behave yourself.

God shall mend my soul! An expression of impatience, corresponding to "God save me!"

mutiny. See note p. 50.

cock-a-hoop, everything in confusion.

you. Said with great scorn.

saucy, insubordinate. A word stronger in meaning then than now.

is't so, indeed? Referring to Tybalt's remark, "'Tis a shame".

trick, *i.e.* sort of behaviour.

scathe, harm.

what, in what way (though I am not going to say). Capulet is obviously hinting that if Tybalt's behaviour does not improve he will find that it will affect his income, or his legacy in Capulet's will.

contrary me, go against my will.

hearts, good fellows. The rest of this speech is interspersed with remarks to the guests.

princox, presumptuous upstart.

cheerly. See note p. 65.

Patience perforce, enforced patience.

choler, anger.

intrusion, *i.e.* of Romeo.

hand. Romeo takes her hand as he says this. The next few speeches are in the form of a Shakespearean sonnet (see note on "PROLOGUE", p. 50). Notice that the recurrence of the rhyming words "this" and "kiss" in ll. 6 and 8 has a binding effect on the two quatrains of the octave, counteracting the separating influence of their being spoken by different people. It is significant that the first words between Romeo and Juliet are in sonnet form, as the sonnet was the accepted form for the language of love (see p. 41).

pilgrims, *i.e.* to the shrine.

wrong. By calling it profane.

faith, *i.e. my* faith.

move, alter, stir from what they know to be right.

my prayer's effect, what is granted in answer to my prayer.

took, taken, as often in Elizabethan English.

trespass, *i.e.* accusation of sin.

Give me my sin again, *i.e.* by kissing me again. "Again" = back again.

by the book, *i.e.* according to a set formula.

What, *i.e.* what position does she hold, what is her family and title.

chinks, cash (from the clatter of the coins).

dear account, sad reckoning. In Elizabethan English the word "dear" intensified the meaning—you could have a "dear friend" and a "dear enemy".

my foe's debt, at the mercy of my foe (because he loves his foe).

is at the best, *i.e.* there is nothing better to come. Another way of putting the proverb, "The game was ne'er so fair", see note on "The game . . . done", p. 62.

the more is my unrest. Realising what dangers there are in his sudden love for Juliet, Romeo applies Benvolio's comment to his own affairs.

foolish. Corresponding to "nothing much".

towards, coming, at hand. (Remember that these guests had been invited to the mask but not to the supper.)

Is it e'en so. Spoken after they had indicated that they were unable to stay any longer. Corresponding to our, "Must you *really* go?"

thank you all, *i.e.* for coming.

Come . . . bed. Not spoken for the hearing of the visitors, of course. Capulet was really glad that they did not wish to stay any longer.

sirrah. Addressed to one of the servants. (See note p. 57.)

fay, faith.

waxes, grows.

What. See note above.

yond, yonder. She points to the first two men merely to hide her interest in the third.

My grave . . . bed, *i.e.* I am not likely to marry anyone else. This, of course, is spoken to herself after the Nurse has gone to enquire the name of the guest.

too late, *i.e.* to make any difference—I cannot help loving him.

Prodigious . . . enemy, (the fate) that I must love a loathed enemy is the portentous birth that love has given to me.

A rhyme. Juliet tells the lie in fear of discovery.

the strangers are all gone. Good manners demand that they stay till then.

Revision Questions on Act I

1. Give an account of the first scene of the Act. What is its connection with the last scene?

2. What is the attitude of (a) Capulet, (b) Lady Capulet to their daughter's marriage to Paris?

3. Describe the first meeting of Romeo and Juliet.

4. Describe the kind of entertainment Capulet planned for his guests.

5. What do you learn of the character of Capulet from this Act?

6. Give examples from the Act of (a) simile, (b) metaphor, (c) circumstantial detail.

7. *So far as you are concerned* do you find the word-play overdone?

Act II. Prologue

PROLOGUE. **Chorus.** See notes p. 50. In this sonnet there is no clear division of thought after the octave.

old desire, *i.e.* Romeo's old love for Rosaline.

young affection. His new love for Juliet.

gapes, eagerly awaits—open-mouthed.

fair, beauty, or beautiful person. The next time the word is used it is an adjective. In Elizabethan English any part of speech was commonly used as another.

for. The second "for" is redundant.

would, was prepared to.

Now . . . again. Benvolio's prophecy has come true (see his last speech in I. ii). His medicine has cured Romeo.

Alike, both equally.

supposed, *i.e.* by the world.

complain, utter his plaints of love. Quite different from the modern sense of the word.

from fearful hooks, *i.e.* at a great risk.

use, are accustomed.

means, means are.

time means, time lends them means.

Tempering extremities, softening, moderating (or mixing) extreme risks.

Act II. Scene i

VERONA: ALANE BY THE WALL
OI= CAPULETS ORCHARD.

On the way home from the mask Romeo has given Benvolio and Mercutio the slip, and he climbs a wall into

Capulet's garden. His two companions call him from the other side of the wall, but, getting no reply, they soon go home to bed.

orchard, garden (not necessarily of fruit trees, though here including them, see ii. 108).

earth, *i.e.* his own earthy body.

centre. If the metaphor of "earth" is continued then the word means the centre of the universe (which the earth was supposed to be) or the centre of the earth. Or (less likely) it may mean the centre of his body, *i.e.* the soul.

Romeo. Benvolio has missed him and is calling him.

conjure. He proceeds to do so in humorous fashion, invoking Romeo in terms suitable for a lover.

humours, passing fancies. See note p. 53.

rhyme. Assumed to be the language of lovers. See note on "hand", p. 66.

'love' and 'dove'. Rhyming words.

gossip Venus, old crony Venus (Roman goddess of love).

purblind, totally blind. See note on "his will", p. 54.

Adam. A stock name for a good archer.

King Cophetua. The story was a favourite ballad topic. Cupid shot "so trim" to bring about so unlikely an occurrence.

in thy likeness, *i.e.* not in a transformed shape.

An if. See note p. 55.

only but. Both words mean the same (as with "an if" above) so that one is redundant. See note on "But saying o'er", p. 56.

humorous, changeable, moody (see note on "humours", above), but punning on the meaning, "humid", "damp".

medlar. A fruit like a small brown apple. The name lent itself to puns, of course.

truckle-bed. Small bed on wheels (*cf.* "truck") which (for a servant) was pushed under a larger bed (the master's). Mercutio means that even a truckle-bed would be better than "this field-bed".

field-bed, camp-bed, here punning on the meaning "lying on the ground".

Go, let us go.

Capulet's Orchard.

ACT II. SCENE II

No sooner have Benvolio and Mercutio gone than over the wall in Capulet's orchard Romeo sees Juliet appear "above at a window" and in the silent night hears her avow her love for him. He reveals his presence, and although somewhat abashed that he has overheard her "true love's passion" she does not withdraw one syllable of it. They exchange "love's faithful vows" and Juliet says that if he will send word at nine o'clock next morning where and at what time their marriage shall take place she will be ready. Romeo sets off for his "ghostly father's cell".

The Nurse's calls add a touch of danger, bringing mild suspense to the meeting of the two lovers—will they be found out?

Some of the language of this scene is very beautiful— "How silver-sweet sound lovers' tongues by night".

He . . . wound. Romeo is no doubt thinking of the scars made by Cupid's arrows, which Mercutio has never felt. This line is obviously a couplet with the previous one, before the change to the scene (not a change in place, however) which Romeo and Juliet have to themselves. The scene division is obviously wrong (see p. 49).

above. See p. 47.

soft! See note p. 54.

envious, jealous Not in the same shade of meaning as on p. 53.

Be not her maid, *i.e.* be not a votary of Diana, a virgin goddess, goddess of the moon—do not continue to live unmarried.

vestal. The priestesses of Vesta, the Roman hearth-goddess, vowed a life of chastity.

sick and green. Shakespeare is probably thinking of the "green-sickness", an anaemic disease causing a lingering death in young women (see III. v. 156).

fools. Perhaps punning on the colours in a jester's motley coat.

were, *i.e.* were my love.

discourses, *i.e.* the language of love.

their spheres, *i.e.* the spheres of the two stars which have gone about "some business".

they in, *i.e.* the stars in.

region, sky.

thou. Romeo and Juliet address one another so ("thou" and "thee") as close friends. See note on "thou's", p. 59. Bear in mind, however, that the address is imaginary to begin with—they do not actually *speak to* one another.

winged messenger, *i.e.* angel.

white-upturned, *i.e.* only the whites of the eyes are seen as they are turned upwards.

wherefore art thou Romeo? And not the son of another family.

Deny. refuse. Both words mean "repudiate", "disown".

this, *i.e.* this point, before she goes any farther.

though not a Montague, even if you were not a Montague, *i.e.* whatever name you go by.

nor . . . nor, neither . . . nor.

owes, owns.

for, *i.e.* in exchange for.

stumblest on my counsel, comes unawares upon my inmost thoughts.

By . . . how, I cannot use my name.

dear saint. *Cf.* Romeo's first words to Juliet (I. v).

thee dislike, displease thee.

o'er-perch, fly over, a metaphor from a bird hopping from perch to perch.

stony limits, boundaries of stone.

dares love. "Love" is the grammatical subject of "dares".

let, deterrent.

proof. Used in the same metaphorical sense as the noun, see p. 54.

but, except. The general sense is, "I would sooner have death with thy love than life without it".

prorogued, deferred, delayed.

wanting of, lacking, being without.

counsel, advice—not the same meaning as in "stumblest on my counsel", above.

I lent him eyes. Cupid is blind (see note on "his will", p. 54).

vast, empty, desolate.

adventure for, speculate in—the regular word for overseas trading in Shakespeare's day. Importing merchants were called "merchant *venturers*".

dwell on form, do the proper thing (in the formal, conventional way).

spoke, spoken. *Cf.* note on "took", p. 67.

compliment, formality.

Jove. King of the Roman gods.

pronounce it faithfully, say what you mean without swearing an oath.

So, provided that, if only.

else, otherwise, *i.e.* I will not do this ("frown and be perverse and say thee nay") *unless* you think that "I am too quickly won".

fond, foolish.

'haviour, behaviour.

light, frivolous, wanton.

cunning to be strange, skill to act in a distant manner.

passion, feeling (of any kind, *e.g.* Christ's "passion"—hence "love's" is added).

Which. The antecedent may be "yielding" or "love". If "light" is the emphatic word in the previous line it would appear to be "yielding", but "discovered" seems to refer to "love". Notice the punning and the antithesis between "light" and "dark".

discovered, revealed (*lit. un*covered).

changes in her circled orb. Referring to the moon's changes within the full circle; or, possibly, to the changes of the moon as it goes through its path in the heavens.

likewise, equally.

gracious, handsome.

Which . . . idolatry, which I worship (as if you were an idol).

contract, *i.e.* of betrothal.

too unadvised, without enough thought.

that, to that heart.

I would . . . again. So that I might have the pleasure all over again.

frank, bountiful, generous.

the thing I have, *i.e.* my love. Explained two and three lines farther on, where she wishes to have it by giving it, for the more she gives the more she has.

Anon. See note p. 63.

substantial, real.

bent, intentions (*lit.* aim, a metaphor from archery).

procure, cause, arrange.

thrive my soul, may my soul prosper.

worse, *i.e.* worse night.

toward, as schoolboys go toward.

Hist! Listen!

tassel-gentle, male of the peregrine falcon. The male falcon was called a "tiercel" because it is smaller than the female by a third: "gentle" (noble) because the peregrine is the noblest kind of falcon.

Bondage is hoarse, *i.e.* my bondage in (a secret) love makes me speak in a whisper.

Echo. A mountain-nymph in Roman mythology (hence "the cave").

make . . . mine. Echo had to speak when anyone else had spoken. "Airy" tongue because an echo has no real voice—the sound comes back on the air.

silver-sweet, *i.e.* as sweet as silver bells.

attending, listening, attentive.

to have, in order to have.

to have thee, so that you may.

any, that I have any.

wanton's bird, pet bird of an irresponsible girl, who (as is shown by what follows) teases her pets.

gyves, fetters (for the legs).

So loving-jealous of his liberty, *i.e.* so fond of the bird that she is jealous of its regaining its liberty.

so sweet, *i.e.* in such sweet places.

ghostly, spiritual (the usual meaning in Elizabethan English, *e.g.* the Holy *Ghost*).

father, *i.e.* his father-confessor—a priest.

dear hap, good fortune. See note on "dear account", p. 67.

ACT II. SCENE III   *FRIAR LAURENCE'S CELL*

In a few hours, as day is breaking, Romeo finds his "ghostly father", Friar Laurence, just about to leave his cell to gather weeds and flowers, in whose medicinal properties he is well-skilled. He is taken aback when Romeo asks to be married that same day, and not to Rosaline, and chides him for being such a waverer. However, he agrees to hear Romeo's story, and sees that one good result of his marriage with a Capulet may be "to turn your households' rancour to true love".

This scene is in rhyming verse (see p. 41). The Friar's first speech is too long for its dramatic purpose—to impress on the audience his skill in making herbal medicines, so that later on the properties of the one he makes for Juliet will be accepted more naturally without disbelief.

Titan. A name sometimes given to the sun-god in Greek mythology.

advance, lift up.

dank, damp.

up-fill. In Elizabethan English it made little difference whether the preposition or adverb came before or after the verb, *e.g.* "my *down*sitting and my *up*rising".

osier cage, willow basket.

ours, *i.e.* the monastery to which he belonged.

baleful, harmful, poisonous.

precious-juiced, *i.e.* containing wonderful properties in their juices.

The earth . . . tomb, *i.e.* all life springs from the earth and when dead goes back to it. The next line contains the same thought, with the two parts in the reverse order.

We. The grammatical subject of the verb "find".

virtues, properties, (medicinal) powers.

but for some, but what are excellent for some "virtue".

mickle, great. The general sense is "great and powerful is the charm".

stones. Shakespeare is probably thinking of minerals, not surface stones.

true, real, when used properly.

strain'd, twisted away.

Revolts . . . abuse, gives up—turns away from—its true nature when it is misapplied. Notice the antithesis in "For nought so vile . . ." and "Nor aught so good . . .", and also in "use" and "abuse".

by action dignified, by the way it is used (presumably in a good cause) becomes dignified.

infant rind, seedling stalk.

medicine. The word may be taken as an adjective describing "power" (*i.e.* medicinal) or (more likely) as a noun (*i.e.* "medicine hath power"). The latter interpretation brings out the antithesis between "poison" and "medicine" more effectively.

that part, *i.e.* its scent.

with the heart, by stopping ("slaying") the heart.

grace and rude will, graciousness and rough obstinacy, self-will.

worser. Double comparatives are another feature of Elizabethan English.

canker, canker-worm.

Benedicite! An ecclesiastical greeting—"Bless (you)" or "Blessed be (God)!"

distemper'd, upset, uneasy, ailing. *Cf.* note on "mistemper'd", p. 52, though the meaning is not the same.

morrow, morning, *i.e.* after one has got up from bed.

keeps his watch, *i.e.* is ever present.

unbruised, *i.e.* by the cares of the world.

unstuff'd, *i.e.* by care (anxiety).

golden, *i.e.* priceless, invaluable.

distemperature, upset of mind (*cf.* the adjective "distemper'd", note above).

that name's woe, *i.e.* the woe Rosaline brought me (by rejecting my suit).

That's my good son. As we say, "That's a good fellow".

feasting, merry-making, celebrating (the emphasis is not on eating and drinking).

mine enemy. The Capulets.

wounded, *i.e.* by love.

both our remedies, the remedy for both of us.

lies. A singular verb to rhyme (in look if not in sound) with "remedies", and not out of place in Elizabethan English, as the idea is singular and also the singular nouns "help" and "physic" immediately precede the verb.

hatred, *i.e.* towards one who is in an "enemy" household.

My intercession likewise steads, what I ask for equally benefits. For "likewise", see note p. 71.

shrift, forgiveness, absolution.

combined, agreed.

combine, unite. The word is used in two senses in the line.

I'll . . . pass. This, of course, is a dramatic necessity, to save repetition of what the audience already knows. "Pass" = walk on.

Saint Francis. Saint Francis of Assisi, the patron saint of his order (the Franciscans).

Maria, Son of Mary.

sallow, *i.e.* making them sallow.

season, preserve (by salt water), the same word as in "seasoning". Salting and drying were the two chief methods of preserving in those (Shakespeare's) days.

it. Probably refers to the seasoning (the "brine").

sighs. Romeo's sighs for Rosaline are thought of as clouds rising into the air. *Cf.* what Romeo says in I. i, "Love is a smoke raised with the fume of sighs".

Lo, here . . . yet. This is not intended to be taken literally, of course.

thyself, *i.e.* true to thyself.

thine, genuine.

sentence, maxim. Not the same meaning as on p. 52.

Women may, *i.e.* no wonder women do.

one, *i.e.* one love.

grace, kindly treatment, graciousness. See note on "grace and rude will", p. 73.

did read . . . spell, had learnt it by heart and could not read, *i.e.* you repeated the words of love without understanding what love meant.

In one respect, for one reason.

To, as to.

stand on, depend on, am in need of.

they stumble that run fast. *Cf.* our proverb, "More haste, less speed".   *THE SAME.*

ACT II. SCENE IV   *A STREET*

At noon the same day Benvolio and Mercutio wonder what has happened to Romeo, especially since he has not been home that night, and put his disappearance down to Rosaline, who "torments him so". They mention that Tybalt has sent Romeo a challenge.

Romeo then meets them and jests with Mercutio in his own mood, which draws from Mercutio the compliment, "Now art thou sociable, now art thou Romeo".

Then the Nurse comes from Juliet, and, after Mercutio and Benvolio have taken the hint and made themselves scarce, Romeo tells her to bid Juliet make some excuse to come for confession to Friar Laurence's cell that same afternoon, and there she shall be married.

man. See note on "men", p. 52, and *cf.* "boy", note p. 66.

pale. Said in disparagement. The Elizabethans (unlike the Victorians) liked their women with a good colour. *Cf.* "white wench" in Mercutio's next speech of any length.

answer. Benvolio means the challenge, Mercutio (quibbling) means the letter.

dared, challenged.

pin, centre-pin. In archery competitions the white target was fastened to a post by a wooden pin: it was thus a sign of extremely good marksmanship to hit the pin in the very centre.

the blind bow-boy. See note on "his will", p. 54.

butt-shaft, arrow used in archery practice at the butts (mounds of earth behind the targets, as used in rifle practice to-day).

man, *i.e.* fit and proper person. Not the same meaning as above.

prince of cats. In the old story of Reynard the Fox the cat is called "Tibert" or "Tybert", a variant of the name Tybalt (Theobald), and it was a name often given to cats (*cf.* the modern "Tibby").

captain of compliments, master of courtly procedure.

prick-song, from music written down (pricked on paper).

proportion, balance, the sequence between one stroke and another.

me. Redundant: an extra word with no meaning after a verb, used in colloquial speech. It simply stands for the person indirectly interested in the fact stated. Not the same use as in "remember'd me", note p. 59.

minim. Continuing the musical metaphor.

butcher of a silk button. The mark of a good duellist, the sort of thing young men used to boast about in those days.

house, rank (of duellists).

of the first and second cause. Causes of duelling, circumstances, according to duelling etiquette, under which a man should lay down a challenge in defence of his honour.

passado! . . . hai! Fencing terms of Italian origin, meaning, respectively, a step forward, a back-handed stroke, the final thrust —from the cry of the duellist as he made it, meaning (in Italian) "You have it". There are many fencing terms in the play— appropriately so.

of, on.

affecting fantasticoes, affected fantastic fellows.

new tuners of accents, speakers in the latest fashion, who affect all the new idioms and mannerisms of speech.

By Jesu. Mercutio now imitates "these new tuners of accents".

blade, fighter (metonymy).

tall, spirited, bold.

grandsire. Said humorously to Benvolio, who is not one of "these new tuners of accents".

flies. Implying that they are always buzzing about.

fashionmongers, followers of (the latest) fashion.

pardonnez-mois, i.e. people who (for effect) bring French expressions into their speech   "Pardonnez-moi" = excuse me. A fulsome politeness is implied.

form. Quibbling on the meaning "bench". *Cf.* the quibble in the antithesis between "stand" and "sit".

bons. "Bon" = good (Fr.). Some editions read "bones", with which it is probably a quibble—after "sit at ease on the old bench".

roe. Punning on his name, and perhaps also on "roe", a female deer, *i.e.* without his lady-love.

fishified, made like a fish.

numbers, (lines of) poetry.

Petrarch. An Italian writer of sonnets (1304-1374) to "Laura".

to, compared to.

Dido. The first of a list of beautiful lovers famous in classical mythology (and Elizabethan literature derived from it). Dido, Queen of Carthage, killed herself when Æneas deserted her.

dowdy, slattern.

Cleopatra a gipsy. Cleopatra was Queen of Egypt (hence "gipsy", with the implication here "dark-skinned"), famous as the lover of Antony, upon whose death she poisoned herself. Shakespeare's *Antony and Cleopatra* is a play on their lives. Cleopatra is, of course, historical (69-30 B.C.).

Helen. The wife of a Grecian king, a woman famed for her beauty, she went off with Paris, son of the King of Troy, and so was the cause of the Trojan War.

Hero. Whose lover, Leander, swam nightly across the Hellespont to see her.

hildings, mean, low women.

Thisbe. Lover of Pyramus. In the face of parental opposition their love ended in a way not unlike that of Romeo and Juliet.

bon jour! Good day (Fr.).

slop, baggy breeches.

counterfeit. Explained by what follows.

slip. A term for counterfeit coin. Here it is used with a double meaning.

great, urgent.

in the hams, *i.e.* awkwardly, or, possibly, very low.

kindly, pertinently.

it, *i.e.* my meaning.

flower. Referring to the phrase, "The flower of courtesy".

pump, court shoe (taking up "courtesy"). A "pinked" shoe was punched with holes in patterns.

follow me this jest, *i.e.* in repartee.

single sole. A pump was made with a single sole, for lightness in dancing (not with a sole added to the shoe, which could be replaced when worn).

sole singular, *i.e.* the bare (soles of the) feet.

single-soled . . . singleness, threadbare jest, only remarkable for its feebleness.

my wits faint, *i.e.* at Romeo's cleverness. (He is being sarcastic, of course.)

Switch, whip.

match, contest. By a metaphor from horse-racing Romeo says, "Let's carry on with the contest—even although your wits faint— or I'll challenge you".

the wild-goose chase, *i.e.* my following you. The term "wild-goose chase" was applied to a contest where two riders started together and as soon as one obtained the lead the other had to follow over the same ground, unless he could overtake him, when the position was reversed. The name is taken from the way a flock of geese flies in a line. The phrase has a rather different meaning now.

was I with you there, did you see my point? Similarly, in a discussion, we say, "Are you with me?"

not there for the goose, not there to play the part of, to act as silly as, a goose. Romeo replies taking "with me" literally.

bite thee by the ear. A term of endearment, not of assault; possibly it arose from the way dogs show their affection for puppies.

bite not. A proverbial saying in those days.

sweeting. A very sweet kind of apple, still grown in Warwickshire. Not surprisingly the word was used metaphorically as a term of endearment. By "bitter sweeting" Mercutio presumably means "good wit, but it is pointed at me".

sauce. Referring to the apple sauce usually served with roast goose.

cheveril, fine kid leather.

it, *i.e.* my wit.

broad goose. Presumably a "big goose".

by art, by skill (in using your wit).

natural, fool, idiot (by derivation—fool by nature).

bauble. The professional fool's token of office, a stick with a fool's head as a mascot on top.

against the hair. Or, as we say, "against the grain", a metaphor from brushing the hair of an animal the opposite way to which it lies. The pun on "tale" (tail) is obvious, of course.

large. Punning on the sense "vulgar", "broad".

occupy the argument, deal with the subject.

goodly gear. Said in reference to the Nurse, who, as she comes, looks like a bundle of clothes. *Cf.* Mercutio's exclamation, "A sail, a sail!".

a shirt and a smock, *i.e.* a man and a woman.

fan. Fans were very large in those days and it was not uncommon for them to be carried by a servant.

God ye, *i.e.* God give you.

good den. See note on "God-den", p. 58.

Is it good den? *i.e.* is it as late as that (after mid-day)?

dial, *i.e.* sun-dial.

made. mar. Antithesis between these two words is common in Shakespeare.

a', he (colloquial).

will . . . sought him. Romeo thinks that she will be wordy.

for fault, in default. Romeo humorously reverses the usual "in default of a better".

took, taken, understood. See note p. 67.

confidence. A malapropism for "conference".

indite. For "invite". He is making fun of the Nurse.

bawd, go-between (Mercutio chooses to imagine for a bad purpose).

hare, woman of loose character.

lenten pie, *i.e.* a poor sort of a pie.

hoar. Referring to the Nurse's grey hairs and punning on the sense "mouldy".

spent, used up.

'lady, lady, lady'. The chorus of an old ballad called *Constant Susanna,* one stanza of which is given in Percy's *Reliques*.

saucy. See note p. 66.

merchant, fellow—in a disparaging sense. Still so used in Warwickshire.

ropery. For "roguery".

take him down. As we say, "Take him down a peg".

an. See note on "an we be in choler", p. 51.

Jacks. The equivalent of "saucy merchants".

Scurvy, vile (the derivation is obvious).

flirt-gills, loose women. "Gill" was a familiar or contemptuous term for a girl (as "Jack" for a boy), *e.g.* the proverb, "Every Jack must have his Gill": and, of course, all readers will be familiar with the nursery rhyme.

skains-mates. The sense is obviously the same as "flirt-gills", and probably "skain" has to do with yarn or thread (skein)—typically a girl's concern.

knave. The word appears here to be nearer the modern sense than when used in I. v (note p. 65). See also two lines from the end of IV. v.

vexed. See note p. 54.

and very weak dealing. This anticlimax is typical of a "weak" intelligence and a wordy tongue—going on for the sake of it.

commend me. Corresponding to our "remember me" (*lit.* recommend me).

Good heart, *i.e.* my good fellow.

thou. Notice that generally (but not invariably) Romeo addresses the Nurse as "thou" and that she addresses him as "you". See note on "thou's", p. 59.

mark, pay attention to.

shrift. See note p. 54.

shrived, absolved from sin (by confession). The verb from "shrift".

Go to, *i.e.* nonsense.

you shall, *i.e.* have it.

tackled stair, rope ladder.

top-gallant. A vessel's "top-gallant sail" is the small sail immediately above the topmast and topsail. The nautical metaphor has been suggested by the "cords made like a tackled stair".

convoy, means of conveyance. This word is not a continuation of a nautical metaphor.

secret. Because dark.

quit, requite.

counsel, a secret.

putting one away, *i.e.* if there is only one there.

lay knife aboard. The general meaning ("win her") is clear, even if the particular metaphor is not. Perhaps the exact metaphor may be rendered "come to table with her".

lieve, gladly.

sometimes. She has not had much chance, since it is not twelve hours since Romeo left Juliet and at that time Juliet did not want the Nurse to know of her affection for Romeo. This shows the little reliance that can be placed upon what the Nurse says. On the other hand, it is by such touches that Shakespeare makes the love of Romeo and Juliet appear of longer growth (see p. 9).

properer, more handsome.

versal, *i.e.* universal.

rosemary. The flower symbolical of remembrance, and hence used at weddings and (see IV. v. 78) at funerals.

that's the dog's name. From the rolling of the *r*, supposed to represent the dog's growling. In his *English Grammar* Ben Jonson wrote, "R is the dog's letter and hirreth in the sound". The Nurse probably gets "name" confused with "letter".

sententious. Malapropism for "sentences" (maxims), see note p. 74.

apace, quickly.

ACT II. SCENE v CAPULETS GARDEN.

At the beginning of the scene Juliet is impatiently awaiting the return of the Nurse, who has been away "three long hours". Just then she comes and, after many grumbles, ultimately conveys the essential information of Romeo's message (given in Scene iv).

Like Friar Laurence's first speech in Scene iii Juliet's first speech here is rather long for its dramatic purpose—to show her anxiety and increase the suspense.

not so, cannot be.
lame. Figuratively speaking, of course.
doves. The chariot of Venus (see note on "gossip Venus", p. 69) was drawn by doves, which were sacred to her.
wind-swift, swift as the wind.
Cupid. See note p. 55.
highmost hill, *i.e.* zenith, highest point in the sky.
affections, passions.
love, *i.e.* lover (not as used previously in the speech).
feign as, act as if.
honey. An adjective.
them. "News" is really a plural word.
give me leave. As we say, "Excuse me".
jaunce, jaunt—which is the word in the First Folio (see pp. 6-7).
circumstance, circumstances, details.
simple, foolish. *Cf.* when we say someone is "a bit simple".
compare, comparison.
hot, passionate.
My back o' t'other side. Spoken as she feels her back.
Beshrew, curse.
jauncing. See note on "jaunce" above. The First Folio again has "jaunting".
Where should she be? *i.e.* where do you expect her to be?
God's lady dear! *i.e.* the Virgin Mary.
marry. See note p. 52.
come up, I trow. A colloquial expression of impatience, as we might say, "Come, come". "I trow" just intensifies it, or lengthens it out; the literal meaning is "I believe".
coil, fuss, to-do. Referring to the fuss the Nurse makes in giving a simple message.
hie, hasten. (The "you" is reflexive.)
be in scarlet, blush (because Juliet has a guilty conscience).
straight. See note p. 61.
ladder. Which Romeo promised his "man" would bring behind the abbey wall.

ACT II.   SCENE vi   *Same Friar Laurence's Cell.*

As arranged, the same afternoon Juliet meets Friar Laurence and Romeo at the Friar's cell, and the Friar says that he "will make short work" of marrying them.

smile the heavens, may the heavens smile.

come what sorrow can, whatever sorrow may come.

countervail, outweigh.

exchange, *i.e.* the exchange of present joy for whatever sorrow may bring in the future.

close, unite.

Then, then let.

I, that I.

triumph, zenith.

Is loathsome in his own deliciousness, *i.e.* it is so sweet that it soon becomes sickly.

confounds, destroys. (*Cf.* the last line of the *Te Deum*, "Let us never be confounded".)

Too swift . . . slow. In the words of our proverb, "More haste, less speed".

gossamer, long single thread of a spider's web.

wanton, playful. The sense is "still air with a gentle puff of wind from time to time".

Good even. See note on "God-den", p. 58.

ghostly. See note p. 72.

thank thee, *i.e.* return your greeting. The Friar says that he will leave Romeo to say good evening (or thank you), implying that Romeo is anxious to speak to her.

As much . . . much, *i.e.* I must say "Good even" to him too, or (if he returns thanks for both of you) his thanks will be too many.

measure, amount.

blazon it, set it forth properly (as on armorial bearings).

neighbour, neighbouring.

rich music's tongue, *i.e.* Juliet's voice.

imagined happiness, happiness of soul.

either, the other.

Conceit, fancy.

ornament, show. Juliet says that the real thing means more to her than any words can say.

worth, *i.e.* wealth (counted in words).

sum up sum, add up the total, *i.e.* I cannot find words to express half my love.

work, *i.e.* work of it.

REVISION QUESTIONS ON ACT II

1. Mention two examples of Romeo's sense of fore-boding, one near the beginning of the Act and one near the end.

2. Give an account of Romeo's visit to the Friar (Sc. iii).

3. Describe a scene where Romeo is in merry mood. What accounts for this change since Act I?

4. Contrast Romeo's talk about Rosaline with that about Juliet.

5. Scene ii is rightly esteemed for its beautiful poetry. Comment on two or three such beautiful passages, quoting where you can.

6. Mention any long speech in Act II which is in rhyming verse and say what you think is the reason for this.

7. Give one important example of suspense in the Act.

ACT III.　Scene i　*A PUBLIC PLACE*

Tybalt, after Romeo's blood, comes upon Mercutio and Benvolio in the street, and Mercutio unwisely fans his anger. Romeo then appears and, following up his challenge, Tybalt calls him a villain, but Romeo speaks him fair and refuses to fight him. Mercutio cannot understand this "vile submission" and invites Tybalt to settle accounts with *him*. Romeo is unable to prevent their fighting, whereupon Mercutio is badly wounded and carried off.

A few minutes later Romeo hears that Mercutio is dead. Then his self-control goes to the winds and he sets about Tybalt and kills him. Another outbreak of street-fighting brings the Prince on the scene. He hears what took place and banishes Romeo forthwith on pain of death.

Mercutio's death is due to his loyalty to Romeo: Tybalt's death is due to Romeo's loyalty to Mercutio. Romeo's banishment now places a new obstacle in the way of the young lovers. Had it not been for a headstrong person in each camp the obstacle would never have arisen. The false sense of honour of Mercutio and Tybalt causes embarrassment for those to whom they are attached.

This scene is the turning point in the play. So far the lovers have had their way. Henceforward their difficulties mount apace.

The day is hot. See note on "quench the fire", p. 65.
abroad, *i.e.* out and about.
scape, escape.
blood, *i.e.* temper, fury. The idea that in hot weather men are more disposed to outbursts of temper is not uncommon in Elizabethan literature, though it seems to have no foundation in fact—rather the reverse

claps me. See note on "me", p. 75.

operation, working (of the drink upon the drinker).

drawer, waiter (who *draws* the liquor from the casks).

Jack. See note p. 78.

moody, bad-tempered. The second time the word is used the sense is "bad-tempered *enough*".

what to? *i.e.* moved to what?

two. Mercutio interprets Benvolio's "to" as "two".

meat, food, not necessarily flesh. *Cf.* the phrase "meat and drink".

as addle, until it is as addled.

tutor me from quarrelling, teach me not to quarrel.

fee-simple of my life, absolute title to ownership of my life (or perhaps my property).

for an hour and a quarter. Implying that by the end of that time he would be dead. (Dramatic irony.)

simple! simpleton!

but, only. See note on "only but", p. 69.

giving, being given one.

thou consort'st with, you keep company with. Notice that at first Tybalt addresses Mercutio as "you", but after Mercutio has angered him he changes to "thou". See note on "thou's", p. 59.

Consort! The regular word for harmony among players, or for an actual group of fiddlers. Out for a quarrel Mercutio gives the word its worst sense—wandering fiddler.

make us minstrels, call us (set us down as) vagabond fiddlers. See note on "give you the minstrel", p. 102.

fiddlestick, *i.e.* his sword.

'Zounds. A contraction of the oath, "By God's wounds" (*i.e.* on the Cross).

coldly, calmly, or, as we say, "coolly".

depart, break up, separate, part yourselves.

not . . . no. See note on "nor . . . no", p. 61.

my man, *i.e.* the man I am looking for. In order to be offensive Mercutio pretends that Tybalt means "my servant" (see note on "men", p. 52).

wear your livery, *i.e.* is your servant.

Marry. See note p. 52.

field, *i.e.* battlefield. Mercutio sarcastically says that Romeo will follow Tybalt (playing on the word "follower") to a place for a fight.

Your worship. Said with great sarcasm.

afford, allow.

the reason . . . thee. His marriage to one of Tybalt's family.

appertaining rage, rage belonging.

know'st me not, dost not know my feelings towards you.

Boy. Here a term of contempt.

injuries, insults (by coming to the mask uninvited—as Tybalt thinks).

devise, imagine.

tender, hold, value.

Alla stoccata, *lit.* to the sword-thrust, *i.e.* the mere *threat* of a duel.

carries it away, wins the day, or, as we say, "gets away with it".

rat-catcher. Because he has a name often given to cats. See note on "prince of cats", p. 75.

will you walk? *i.e.* to a quiet place where we may fight a duel.

nine lives. Proverbially cats have nine lives.

make bold withal, take, make free with.

as you shall use me hereafter, according to the way in which you treat me after I have taken one of your nine lives, *i.e.* the way I feel after fighting with you.

dry-beat, beat till they are dry.

pilcher, scabbard.

ears, *i.e.* hilt. "By the ears" was a contemptuous expression in Shakespeare's day.

for, ready for.

passado. See note p. 76.

bandying, exchanging blows.

sped, finished with.

nothing, *i.e.* no hurt.

villain. Said affectionately, of course, not in the way in which Tybalt calls Romeo a "villain", but just as to-day people playfully say, "You rascal".

peppered, done for, "sped".

'Zounds. See note p. 83.

a dog . . . a cat. These metaphors are applied to Tybalt.

by the book of arithmetic, *i.e.* according to a set plan. Mercutio has previously said that in his fighting Tybalt "keeps time, distance, and proportion".

all, *i.e.* all I did.

I have it. We have the same sense in our current slang—"I've had it".

ally, kinsman.

very, own close.

With Tybalt's slander. "Thou art a villain."

temper, temperament, punning on the "temper" of steel.

aspired, risen to.

untimely, prematurely.

on more days doth depend, hangs over other days (in the future).

others, *i.e.* other woes.

respective, respectful.

conduct, conductor, guiding principle.

take the villain back again, I hurl your slander (calling me villain) back again in your teeth.

consort. See note on "thou consort'st with", p. 83.

Shalt, shalt go.

up, *i.e.* in arms, in a rabble.

doom thee death, pass sentence of death on you. "Doom" = judge. In the Isle of Man a judge is still called a "deemster".

fortune's fool, the sport of fortune, made a mockery.

First Cit. This man speaks with authority and is obviously more than an ordinary private citizen happening to be passing at the time. In some editions he is called "Captain", and this is more fitting his part.

Up, come on.

discover, reveal, disclose, *lit. un*cover.

manage, course, management.

my cousin! O my brother's child! "Cousin" was used loosely of any relationship, and, indeed, even between friends, in Elizabethan times.

O cousin! There is no need to consider whom Lady Capulet is addressing here. She is distraught, and this exclamation clearly refers to Tybalt. Some editors omit it, as the line is too long, and consider its inclusion due to a printer's copying of the word from the previous line.

true, just.

nice, petty, trivial, punctilious, founded, as we say, on a "nice point of honour".

withal, in addition, thereto.

take, make.

spleen, anger.

that. Unnecessary to the sense of the line. It merely gives emphasis.

hot, *i.e.* hot-tempered.

Cold death, *i.e.* Tybalt's sword.

Retorts it, turns its back.

he. Like "that" above merely for emphasis. One might paraphrase it "for his part".

envious, malicious. Still another shade of meaning for this word (*cf.* notes pp. 53 and 70).

hit. fled. Apart from these verbs Benvolio's account of the fight is in the present tense, up to "was stout Tybalt slain".

entertain'd, thought of, harboured the idea of (as one "entertains" a guest, or "entertains" an idea).

owe, possess, *i.e.* who is to pay for his death with his own life?

concludes, ends, *i.e.* he has only taken the law into his own hands.

we. The Prince is here speaking in his official capacity and uses the royal "we". In the next line he is referring to a personal matter and says "I".

interest, *i.e.* personal interest.

your hate's proceeding, action that has proceeded from your hate.

My blood. Mercutio was the Prince's kinsman.

amerce you with so strong, punish you with so heavy.

the loss of mine, my loss.

purchase out, buy out, redeem.

attend our will, wait on "us" to do what "we" require, or, perhaps, pay attention to what "we" have decided.

Mercy . . . kill, giving pardon to murderers only causes more murders to take place. "Pardoning" = when it pardons.

Act III.   Scene ii

Daylight seems slow departing as Juliet waits impatiently (*cf.* the beginning of II. v) for the arrival of Romeo on their wedding night.   But the mood changes suddenly when the Nurse brings news of Tybalt's death and Romeo's banishment in consequence.   Juliet is at first distraught with conflicting emotions, but she soon realises that Romeo must have been defending his life.   Not till the end of the scene does the Nurse disclose that Romeo is hidden at Friar Laurence's cell, and Juliet sends to him to "bid him come to take his last farewell", with her ring as a token.

Compare Juliet's first speech in the scene with her first speech in Act II, Scene v. The dramatic purpose of both is the same, and here there is added the contrast between her hopes and what the future really holds.

you fiery-footed steeds.   That draw the chariot of the sun-god (Phœbus) through the sky.

Phœbus.   The Roman sun-god, also called Apollo.

Phæthon.   Son of the sun-god, was allowed to take charge of his father's chariot for one day, but he drove so wildly that the horses rushed out of the usual track and came too near the earth, which would have been set on fire had not Jupiter (king of the gods) hurled a thunderbolt at the charioteer.

love-performing, *i.e.* making it easy for lovers.

runaways' eyes may wink.   The first word is variously printed in different editions, with and without the apostrophe, and with the apostrophe before and after the *s*.   Whatever the exact reading should be, the general sense is clear from the next line, that the eyes of people who might see Romeo shall be closed. "Wink" = close, be unable to see.

if love be blind.   See note on "his will", p. 54.

civil, grave, serious, "sober-suited", the opposite of showy.

learn.   See note p. 63.

lose a winning match, *i.e.* by losing her "maidenhood" she will win a husband.

hood my unmann'd blood.   A metaphor from falconry.   A hood was put over the eyes of a hawk until the prey was sighted. "Unmann'd", *i.e.* untrained to the presence of man, when it "bated" or kept fluttering on the wrist if its eyes were not covered. There is, of course, a pun on "unmann'd".

till strange . . . modesty, till my reserve grows cold (or is broken down) and thinks the actions of true love a very ordinary thing.   "Strange" = reserved.

day, *i.e.* bright joy.

black-brow'd.   It was unfashionable for women to be dark in

Queen Elizabeth I's reign, as the Queen herself was fair (sandy), but Juliet welcomes a dark night.

when he (I) shall die. The reading "I" makes better sense. Surely Juliet would not think of Romeo's death now! The implication is that when she is gone she does not want any other woman to enjoy him, but "all the world", which is more in line with feminine feeling.

fine, *i.e.* bright.

garish, gaudy, glaring.

I am sold. Continuing the metaphor of the empty house in reverse. She has sold herself to Romeo, but he has not yet entered into possession.

well-a-day. A corruption of an Old English exclamation of woe. Similar to "alas the day" (an intensified form of "alas"), l. 72, and "alack the day", IV. v. 22.

envious. See note p. 85.

'I', *i.e.* ay. The word was often printed thus (following its sound) in old texts.

cockatrice. A creature fabled to kill by a look, said to be like a serpent with a cock's head; often identified with the basilisk.

those eyes, *i.e.* Romeo's eyes.

Brief sounds determine of, let brief sounds decide.

weal, welfare.

God save the mark! An exclamation, possibly (1) from the prayer of an expectant mother for her child ("God prevent the birth-mark!"), or (2) a mother's prayer after the child had been born with a birth-mark, meaning "God prevent the mark having any ill effect", either of which would be very appropriate exclamations for a nurse. The mark may possibly just mean the sign of the Cross, but it is not so likely in this context.

gore-blood, clotted blood.

swounded, swooned.

bankrupt. Having lost all it possessed.

Vile earth. Addressing her own body.

resign, *i.e.* resign yourself.

heavy. Because it has the weight of *two* bodies.

so contrary, *i.e.* in opposite directions.

the general doom, *i.e.* for the world's Day of Judgment.

O serpent . . . face! Like a serpent under a flower, a comparison Shakespeare uses again in *Macbeth*.

keep, live in, dwell in.

Beautiful tyrant! This pairing of opposites and the others which follow are further examples of oxymoron (see note on "loving hate", p. 54).

show, appearance.

Just, exact.

justly, rightly. The word is used in a different sense from "just" above. Juliet plays upon the word.

hadst thou to do, were you about.

bower, embower, enclose.

book . . . bound. A metaphor Lady Capulet had used (of a *good* book, however) when describing Paris (see her long speech in I. iii).

naught, worthless, good-for-nothing. A much stronger word then than the present-day "naughty".

where's my man? Notice the irony—very humorous on the stage: in one breath she condemns men, in the next she asks for her own "man" (servant).

aqua vitæ, brandy.

may, *i.e.* may rightly.

That villain . . . husband. Her intuition gives her the answer to her own question. "Villain" is here an adjective.

that, whom (the object of "would have slain").

worser. See note p. 73.

presses to, forces itself on.

Hath slain, *i.e.* on balance is equal to the death of.

needly . . . griefs. As we say, "If griefs never come singly". "Needly will" = must needs.

modern, ordinary, common. (*Cf.* "modesty", note on "till strange . . . modesty", p. 86.) "Modern lamentation" is the object of the verb "might have moved" ("which" its subject).

rearward, piece of news tacked on at the end. Metaphor from the rearguard of an army.

Is, *i.e.* is equal to.

that word, *i.e.* the word "banished".

sound. A metaphor from navigation—measure the depth of, doubtless with a play on the other meaning (utter) as well.

corse, corpse.

Wash they, they can wash.

spent, poured out. Not the meaning in note p. 78.

beguiled, cheated (of your purpose).

I'll to my wedding-bed. *Cf.* her speech near the end of I. v— "My grave is like to be my wedding-bed".

wot, know.

ACT III.   SCENE III

FRIAR LAURENCE'S CELL

In Friar Laurence's cell (whither he has fled after killing Tybalt) Romeo hears from the Friar the Prince's doom of banishment. He acts in frenzied fashion, but the Friar brings him to himself, and in practical fashion advises him to go and live in Mantua.

Meanwhile the Nurse has come (her knock on the door adds to the suspense—is Romeo's hiding-place discovered?). Before the end of her visit she gives Juliet's message—after a fashion, together with the ring, and Romeo's "comfort" is much "revived" to know that she still wants him.

thou. Notice how the Friar, on terms of familiarity with Romeo, his spiritual pupil, addresses him as "thou". When he bids him farewell, however, it is "you", probably because he feels that it is a formal courtesy or perhaps because the official interview is over and he feels that he is no longer speaking as Romeo's "ghostly father". When the Nurse comes in she addresses Romeo as "you", but he addresses her (as a servant) as "thou". See note on "thou's", p. 59.

fearful, full of fear—the literal meaning.

parts, (good) qualities.

doom, judgment, sentence. *Cf.* note on "doom thee death", p. 84.

acquaintance at my hand, my acquaintance.

Too familiar . . . company. The Friar implies that he is bringing *good* news.

dooms-day, death, *lit.* judgment-day (see note on "doom", above).

vanished. A curious word, but the sense seems to be that the judgment has gone from his lips with the breath that uttered it.

Verona. See note p. 50.

without, outside. *Cf.* the hymn,

> There is a green hill far away,
> *Without* a city wall.

world's exile, exile *from* the world.

mis-term'd, miscalled.

with a golden axe, *i.e.* you call it by a more attractive name, but the effect is just as deadly: in other words, you use a euphemism.

death, *i.e.* as a punishment.

rush'd. The word contains an idea of quickly and arbitrarily pushing aside.

validity, value.

courtship, "honourable state" at court, with a pun on its modern sense, no doubt.

vestal. See note p. 70.

mean, means.

ghostly. See note p. 72.

fond. See note p. 71.

sweet milk, *i.e.* it makes adversity palatable.

Hang up, *i.e.* get rid of (as the hangman gets rid of a criminal).

Displant, *i.e.* take it up and plant it somewhere else.

dispute, talk (it over).

estate, situation.

An hour but, only an hour. See note on "only but", p. 69.

infold me, enfold me, wrap me up.

Who's there? Shouted to the person outside. *Cf.* "By and by!" "I come . . .''

simpleness, folly (referring to Romeo's tantrums). *Cf.* note on "simple", p. 80.

case, state.

Blubbering. There is no contemptuous slant in the meaning of the word.

O, *i.e.* groaning "O".

death's the end of all, *i.e.* we all have to die some day.

old, confirmed.

the childhood. In antithesis with "old".

My conceal'd lady, *i.e.* the fact that she is his lady is concealed.

deadly level of a gun, gun levelled with deadly aim.

this anatomy, *i.e.* his own body.

lodge, dwell.

cries out, *i.e.* announces, proclaims.

Unseemly, *i.e.* unseemly in a man.

both, *i.e.* a man in form and a woman in the way you take misfortune.

amazed, astounded, dumbfounded. A much stronger word in Elizabethan English than now.

my holy order. The Franciscan Order (of monks). See note on "Saint Francis", p. 74.

temper'd, mixed, made up (as steel is made of a certain "temper"). *Cf.* note on "Tempering extremities", p. 68.

Why rail'st thou on thy birth. Romeo has not done so, but the Romeus of Brooke's poem did, and Shakespeare has here followed his source inconsistently with his play.

meet in thee at once, have a place in you at the same time, "heaven and earth" here meaning soul and body.

wit. See note p. 62.

Which abound'st in all, all of which abound in you.

like a usurer. Because you have them but hoard them. The simile also refers to the next two lines. Notice the play on "usurer", "usest", "use".

Digressing, departing.

love, loved one, *i.e.* he would kill Juliet (metaphorically speaking) by his own death.

that ornament, *i.e.* it is well-suited to his "shape (form) and love".

conduct, ruling, governance.

flask. Old-time soldiers carried their powder in wooden "flasks".

dismember'd with, blown to pieces by the means of. Romeo's "wit", properly used, should be the means of protecting (not destroying) him.

dead, *i.e.* ready to die.

There, in that.

would, wanted to.

decreed, determined, decided.

Ascend. It had been arranged that he should ascend to Juliet's room by a rope-ladder.

hence, go hence.

the watch. See p. 18.

Mantua. See note p. 59.

blaze, publish abroad.

heavy sorrow. On account of Tybalt's death.

How well . . . this! The fact that Juliet has sent him a ring shows that she still loves him although he has slain her kinsman.

here stands all your state, all your fortune depends on this.

signify, make known to you.

Every good hap, everything that happens favourable.
brief, briefly, *i.e.* with so few words. *A room in Capulet's house.*

ACT III. SCENE IV

Capulet tells Paris that he shall marry Juliet on the following Thursday (three days later).

Here we see difficulties mounting up for Juliet parallel to those of Romeo.

move, persuade.
promise, assure.
woe. woo. A play upon words, as they were pronounced alike.
know, find out, discover.
mew'd up to her heaviness, caged up in her grief. See pp. 42-43. A metaphor from falconry: the hawk was put in a "mew" when she cast her feathers.
desperate tender, venturesome offer. "Desperate" because he has not yet had Juliet's consent.
ere you go to bed. It would appear that Lady Capulet left it until next morning, unless, of course, she did not go to bed till morning (see Capulet's last words in the scene).
my son. In Elizabethan England engaged couples commonly called their future in-laws father or mother (and were themselves called son or daughter) *before* marriage. Capulet is thus not anticipating events, as it seems to us.
ha, ha! Not laughter, but just expressing hesitation.
O', on.
keep no great ado, make no big fuss.
late, recently, lately.
carelessly, without regard.
Being, since he was.
against, in readiness for.
Afore me! before me, a petty oath, weakened from "Afore God!". It is not so likely that it means "Carry light before me", or that he is politely telling Paris to go before him as they leave.

ACT III. SCENE V *Juliet's chamber.*

At the beginning of the scene Romeo and Juliet are bidding one another farewell (on the balcony outside her window) after their one night together before Romeo leaves for banishment.

The Nurse comes to tell Juliet to be careful as it is daybreak and her mother is on the way to her room (see Sc. iv). At this Romeo cannot delay any longer and quickly drops to the ground.

Lady Capulet brings Juliet the news that her marriage to Paris has been arranged to take place in three days' time.

Capulet follows her, and he is angry and abusive at Juliet's unwillingness: he will take no refusal and tells her that she can either marry Paris or be turned out of house and home without a penny.

After her parents have gone Juliet finds that there is no possibility of comfort from the Nurse and determines to go and see Friar Laurence.

In this scene Romeo and Juliet see one another alive for the last time.

Notice the contrast between the beauty of the lovers' parting words and the harshness of the wrangling which follows, between Juliet's loyal love and the Nurse's worldly wisdom.

Throughout her conversation with her mother Juliet speaks with double meaning and her words are full of dramatic irony.

The scene is conventionally given as "Capulet's Orchard". Scenes did not matter to Shakespeare, whose stage was practically without scenery (see p. 46), but it is quite obvious that there are two "scenes" here—the first where Romeo and Juliet are "above" to begin with (see p. 47) and later talk to one another after Romeo's descent into the garden by the rope-ladder, the second where the "scene" is Juliet's bedroom.

    above. See p. 47.
    Wilt, *i.e.* must.
    thou. See note p. 70.
    fearful. Sounds make him fearful because he dreads discovery by day.
    lace. A metaphor from lace-work.
    severing, separating.
    Night's candles, *i.e.* the stars.
    tiptoe, *i.e.* ready to spring forth.
    I. Added for emphasis.
    meteor that the sun exhales. Meteors were thought to be caused by the rays of the sun igniting vapours drawn up ("exhaled") from the earth by the sun's warmth. In *Henry IV, Part I*, Shakespeare calls meteors "exhalations".
    so, if, provided that.
    reflex, reflection.
    Cynthia. A name for the moon in classical mythology.
    Nor . . . not. See note on "Nor no", p. 61.
    care, wish, desire.
    will, determination.
    my soul. Spoken to Juliet.

Straining, *i.e.* straining her voice so that it produces.

division, trilling sound. On an instrument like a harp it is impossible to play a long note, so the note was said to be "divided" into a succession of shorter notes to give a similar effect. The pun with "divideth" is obvious.

the lark . . . eyes. A rustic fancy because the toad's eyes are beautiful and the lark's small and unattractive.

I would . . . too! For the toad's croak would be no "herald of the morn".

affray, frighten us. The verb now survives only in the past participle—"afraid".

hunt's-up, a morning song or greeting. The name was derived, of course, from the huntsman's early morning song.

broke, broken. *Cf.* note on "took", p. 67, and "spoke", p. 71.

in a minute there are many days, *i.e.* a minute of your absence will seem as long as many days to me.

count, reckoning.

ill-divining soul, soul foreboding evil. See p. 16.

Dry sorrow drinks our blood. Another old belief, that sorrow caused people to go pale through lack of blood.

dost thou, is your concern.

down, *i.e.* gone to bed—to lie down.

up, *i.e.* is she up.

procures her, makes her come. *Cf.* note p. 72.

how now, *i.e.* what's the matter?

some. The emphatic word (in antithesis with "much of" in the next line).

feeling, deeply felt. She really means Romeo, though she knows Lady Capulet will take it to refer to Tybalt. See p. 92.

but not, but not feel, *i.e.* your grief will not bring back the friend whom you mourn.

weep, weep for.

thou weep'st . . . him. Lady Capulet gives this as *her* opinion (trying to divert Juliet's attention from what she supposes to be her grief for Tybalt). Notice that in her conversation with her daughter when Lady Capulet gets familiar she addresses her as "thou": Juliet, however, always keeps the more respectful "you".

like he, like him—to be grammatically correct.

traitor. An adjective.

venge, avenge.

runagate, vagabond, runaway.

unaccustom'd dram, *i.e.* dram to which he is unaccustomed (poison).

—dead—. Juliet's *real* meaning (not the one for her mother) is "Dead is my poor heart", and the "kinsman" may be Romeo, or she may mean that she is "vex'd" for Tybalt's death because it has taken Romeo from her.

temper. See note p. 90.

his body that, the body of the man that. Juliet's real meaning in all this speech should be followed, as well as her superficial meaning.

needy, *i.e.* needy of joyful tidings.

careful, *i.e.* one who cares for you—the literal meaning.

sorted out a sudden day, arranged an unexpected day (as in the next line).

County. See note p. 58.

These are news. Said sarcastically, referring to the "joyful tidings".

your. When Lady Capulet is annoyed she addresses Juliet more formally ("your" not "thy").

at your hands, *i.e.* from you yourself (from your own lips).

Who. The antecedent is "thy sighs".

calm, *i.e.* succeeding them.

decree, decision. *Cf.* note on "decreed", p. 90.

she will . . . thanks, she declines with thanks. In view of Capulet's next words, "Doth she not give us thanks?" Lady Capulet's meaning may be, "She gives you thanks—and nothing else!".

take me with you, let me understand you.

proud, *i.e.* of such a marriage.

her, herself. *Cf.* note on "remember'd me", p. 59.

wrought, arranged for.

thankful, *i.e.* in so far as you have done it out of love for me.

meant love, meant to be love, done with a loving motive.

How now. See note p. 59.

chop-logic, quibbler, splitting hairs.

minion, spoilt child.

Thank . . . prouds, *i.e.* do not argue with me. A common method of rebuff in Shakespeare's time.

fettle, get ready, get in good trim.

'gainst. See note on "against", p. 91.

hurdle. A wooden framework in which prisoners were taken to punishment.

green-sickness. See note on "sick and green", p. 70.

baggage, good-for-nothing. A contemptuous term.

tallow-face. See note on "pale", p. 75.

are you mad? Lady Capulet may be joining in the attack on Juliet or (in view of her next speech) she may think that her husband is going too far.

Hang thee, hang thyself. *Cf.* note on "her", above.

after, afterwards.

itch, *i.e.* to hit you.

hilding. See note p. 76.

rate, scold.

smatter, chatter, utter your smatterings of wisdom and prudence.

gossips. See note on "gossip Venus", p. 69.

God ye god-den. See notes pp. 58 and 78. This appears to be spoken in impatience, not as an actual farewell nor as a polite way of telling her to go, though Capulet himself does go out before long.

hot, hot-tempered.

God's bread, *i.e.* in the Sacrament.

tide. An old word for "time", now surviving in the phrase

"time and tide" and in the name of certain festivals, *e.g.*
Whitsun*tide*.

Stuff'd, crammed full.

puling, "whining".

mammet, puppet.

in her fortune's tender, when (good) fortune makes her an offer.

Graze, *i.e.* feed

do not use, am not accustomed.

lay hand on heart, advise, seriously consider, be careful.

Nor . . . never. See note on "Nor no", p. 61.

Trust to 't, *i.e.* I mean it, you can rely on what I say.

be forsworn, go back on my word.

I'll not speak a word, *i.e.* in your favour to your father.

thou. Here used not in friendly fashion, but for a less respectful and more contemptuous address. See note on "thou weep'st
. . . him", p. 93.

my faith, all I believe in. The method of expression of the
passage in which these words occur, bringing out the antithesis
between "earth" and "heaven", makes it involved, but the general
idea is very simple—there is no solution so long as Romeo remains
alive.

practise, plot.

all the world, *i.e.* I stake all the world.

challenge, claim

dishclout, washing-up cloth. A common term of abuse in
Elizabethan English.

green. Green eyes were much admired in Southern Europe.

Beshrew. See note p. 80.

living . . . use, your living here and having no use.

Amen! Juliet confirms the Nurse's curse on her heart and soul
—"beshrew them both".

Well . . . much. Juliet sees that she can get no help from
the Nurse, and so determines to go to Friar Laurence. These
words are not spoken in a tone of bitter sarcasm, rather of utter
despair; perhaps, however, they may be spoken in an assumed
brightness, so as to allay suspicions arising from the Nurse's
"What?".

Ancient damnation! the old devil!

forsworn. She is referring to her marriage vows.

above compare, as above comparison. The "with" preceding
goes with the relative pronoun "which"—"with which . . .".

Thou . . . twain, *i.e.* I shall not come to you for counsel any
more, we two must go our own separate ways.

Revision Questions on Act III

1. Describe how (*a*) Mercutio, (*b*) Tybalt met their
deaths.

2. What is your opinion of (*a*) Romeo's conduct in the
Friar's cell, (*b*) Capulet's conduct when he finds out that
Juliet is unwilling to marry Paris?

3. Give examples of the way the Nurse carries messages or gives information.

4. Mention any speeches or episodes which increase the suspense of the audience.

5. Quote or refer to any passages in Scene v which forebode ill. What is their dramatic importance?

ACT IV. SCENE I *Friar Laurence's Cell.*

When Juliet gets to Friar Laurence's cell she finds Paris there making arrangements for their wedding. She speaks to him with tolerable courtesy, and he treats her kindly but without any rapture in his love (perhaps we should not expect it before the Friar). After a little while she gives him the hint to go. This is the only time in the play that Juliet and Paris meet.

The door is no sooner shut behind him than she gives way to her distress, but the Friar counsels her to "go home, be merry" and "consent to marry Paris". He then gives her a potion of "distilled liquor", to be taken after she has gone to bed. It shall, he says, simulate death for forty-two hours, covering her marriage morning. Instead of marrying Paris she shall be carried to "that same ancient vault where all the kindred of the Capulets lie", whither shall Romeo be summoned "by my letters" to "watch thy waking, and that very night shall Romeo bear thee hence to Mantua". Juliet is all for the Friar's plan.

The Friar's last speech but one is again (see p. 73) somewhat long for its dramatic purpose.

My father. See note on "my son", p. 91.
to slack, so as to slacken.
Uneven, irregular.
Venus. See note on "gossip Venus", p. 69.
minded, *i.e.* in her mind.
society, company.
why it should be slow'd. The fact that Juliet was already married, of course.
That may be, that which may be.
To answer, in answering.
price, value.
spoke. See note p. 71.
abused, spoilt.
Thou. Notice that when Paris starts to speak in tender fashion to Juliet he addresses her as "thou". *Cf.* note p. 95.

tears, tears do.

to my face. Spoken with a double meaning; (1) openly, (2) about my face.

it is not mine own. Her hidden meaning is that it is Romeo's.

Are you . . . mass? A polite hint to Paris that she wishes to be alone with the Friar.

pensive, sad, melancholy—a stronger word than now.

shield, forbid, prevent.

O, shut . . . help! Notice that all these words are monosyllables. Simplicity is the mark of real feeling: insincerity disguises itself in wordy language.

prorogue. See note p. 71.

resolution, *i.e.* to commit suicide.

help it, *i.e.* "help my resolution", perhaps "further your wise advice".

presently, at once—the literal meaning of the word.

label, "seal". In Shakespeare's day seals were attached to documents by strips called "labels".

deed. Euphemism.

both, *i.e.* heart and hand.

long-experienced time, long lifetime of experience.

present, immediate (*cf.* "presently", above).

extremes, extremities of suffering.

play the umpire, *i.e.* decide between them.

arbitrating . . . bring, deciding that which the authority of your years and knowledge could not honourably settle.

to speak, in speaking. *Cf.* "To answer", above.

Hold. Notice that the Friar's next two speeches after this one also begin with this word. It was not an uncommon exclamation. A rendering in modern English would be "Here!".

craves as desperate an execution, needs action as desperate in carrying it out.

chide, drive. *Lit.* by words, but not here.

cop'st, meetest.

thievish, *i.e.* where thieves abound.

O'er-cover'd. The Elizabethans were not so particular as we are whether the preposition came before or after the verb, *e.g.* "my down-sitting and my up-rising".

reeky, rotting, *lit.* smoky.

chapless, fleshless, *lit.* jawless.

to hear, *i.e.* just to hear.

look, see.

lie, sleep.

being then in bed, *i.e.* after you have got into bed.

humour, feeling. *Cf.* note p. 53.

his native progress, but surcease, its natural progress, but shall cease. In Elizabethan English "his" was the neuter as well as the masculine possessive adjective.

paly, palish.

thy eyes' windows, *i.e.* the lights in your eyes.

supple government, the control which makes it supple.

stark, rigid, "stiff".

appear like death. No such drug is, of course, known to medicine or science.

two and forty hours. Actually the period of Juliet's "sleep" did not tally with the Friar's estimate. See p. 14.

as the manner of our country is. Stated because this was an Italian, not an English, custom. See pp. 17-18.

uncover'd on the bier, *i.e.* not in a coffin.

against thou shalt awake, in readiness for thy awakening. For "against" see note p. 91.

drift, purpose, plan.

inconstant toy, unsettling trifle.

tell not me, do not talk to me.

help, *i.e.* the "remedy".

ACT IV.   SCENE II

HALL IN CAPULETS HOUSE

Capulet is bustling about with preparations for the wedding breakfast. His idea of a quiet wedding has evidently been abandoned (see p. 33).

His heart is "wondrous light" when Juliet returns from Friar Laurence in repentant submission and he puts the wedding forward to Wednesday, notwithstanding his wife's fears that they will be "short in their provision".

Sirrah. See note p. 57.

cunning, skilful. *Cf.* note on "cunning to be strange", p. 71. Here the word is an adjective, however.

'tis . . . fingers. The implication being that he does not wish to taste his own dishes.

unfurnish'd, unprepared.

becomed, becoming.

stepping o'er. *Cf.* note on "o'er-cover'd", p. 97.

afore God! See note on "Afore me!", p. 91.

this reverend . . . him. There is a change of construction in the middle of the sentence.

furnish me, prepare me for. *Cf.* note on "unfurnish'd", above.

provision. This refers to all the arrangements for the wedding, not just food (although it includes the food).

stir about. In modern idiom, "get moving".

let me alone, *i.e.* leave things to me.

forth, *i.e.* out. "They" refers to the servants, of course.

reclaim'd. Another metaphor from falconry. To "reclaim" a hawk was to recall it, or entice it back.

ACT IV.   SCENE III

Juliets Chamber.

Juliet takes the Friar's potion last thing at night—not without fearful misgivings.

The charnel beauty of her soliloquy here should be compared with the fragrant beauty of her speeches in Act II.

attires, dresses (a noun).

state, *i.e.* of heart and mind, as is evident from the next line.

cross, "wayward".

behoveful for our state, necessary for our (appearance in) state. "State" here has a different meaning from that above.

So please you, if you please.

all, entirely.

What should she do, *i.e.* what good would she be?

minister'd, prepared, provided.

should not, is not likely to (be a poison).

still. See note p. 54.

tried, proved.

healthsome, wholesome.

strangled, suffocated.

conceit, idea, fancy.

As, being, namely, that is.

green, *i.e.* fresh.

festering, rotting.

like, likely.

mandrakes' torn, *i.e.* mandrakes' shrieks when they (the mandrakes) are torn. The mandrake has a forked root, in popular imagination supposed to resemble a man or a duck (*man-drake*), and as it was used as a sleep-giving drug a number of superstitions clung about it. One was that it shrieked if torn out of the ground and the person who had pulled it went mad at the sound.

distraught, distracted, mad.

my cousin. Tybalt.

spit, *i.e.* transfix, pierce through, as meat for roasting before the fire was impaled on a spit (see the next scene).

stay, stop, do not do it.

this do I drink to thee. She takes the Friar's potion as if drinking Romeo's health, thinking, in her imagination, to go to him when he needs her.

ACT IV. SCENE IV

[Hall in Capulet's house.]

This short scene shows the early morning hurry and bustle preparatory to the wedding. At the end the arrival of the bridegroom is announced.

A scene in a play may do one or more of the following:

1. Advance the plot.

2. Create an atmosphere.

3. Develop a character.

4. Give dramatic relief—contrast.

5. Make an impression of the flight of time between two other scenes.

Nothing is added to the plot by this scene, but its value is as a side-scene in contrast to the main theme. In the previous scene there was Juliet's terror as she prepared to take the potion; we last saw her upon her bed after taking it. We imagine her there still as death: meanwhile in a different part of the house everyone is running to and fro in a great haste. The scene creates an atmosphere, an atmosphere of complete contrast to the terror and stillness before and the lamentation afterwards, giving dramatic relief. In addition it gives the impression of the passing of time through the night between Juliet's bedtime and early morning.

The delay to the progress of the plot heightens the suspense: all the time the audience is waiting to see what will happen when Juliet is discovered (to all appearances) dead.

Further, a scene like this helps to bring the main events into touch with ordinary life. The transformation of Juliet is not so unbelievable, so far removed from the life of this world, when it happens in a household like this. We are given a sense that it is not happening in an unreal world, far away, but in "the world which is the world of all of us".

pastry, the room where the paste (pastry) was made. *Cf.* "pantry", where the bread (Fr. "pain") was made.

curfew-bell. Not to be taken literally, of course; simply the alarm bell to wake the servants.

cot-quean, *lit.* queen of a cot (a labourer's cottage), a term disparagingly applied to a man who did the household chores. Some critics think that this speech should be given to Lady Capulet, as the Nurse would not dare to take the liberty of addressing her master thus. It all depends on who Angelica is; certainly a remark like "Spare not for cost" would be more fittingly addressed to his wife. As against this, in the first quarto the speech is unmistakably the Nurse's, for Capulet replies, "I warrant thee, Nurse . . .". And it must be remembered that the day of Juliet's wedding would be a day when an old family servant who had been her nurse since she was born might be allowed some liberties. At all events the Nurse was not the type of person to be slow taking them.

sick, ill.

watching, keeping awake—as in "Watch and pray".

mouse-hunt, runner after women. "Mouse" was a term of endearment to women in Shakespeare's time, *e.g.* in *Twelfth Night* the Clown calls his mistress "my mouse of virtue", and the word is used in this sense in *Hamlet*.

logger-head, blockhead (*lit. log*-head).

music straight, *i.e* musicians straightway. In Old England bride and bridegroom did not meet at the church. It was the custom for the bridegroom to call early for the bride to take her to church—with music in well-to-do families.

For . . . would. He said so to Juliet too (IV. i. 42)—assuming that the wedding would be on Thursday.

the bridegroom he is come already. Yet a few minutes before it was only three o'clock (l. 4). Such discrepancies, however, would not be noticed by an audience so much as by the student with the book before him. Shakespeare no doubt intended to give the impression of the night's being passed in preparation for the morrow's festivities. In any event he was never very particular about details.

ACT IV. SCENE V   *Juliets chamber.*

At daybreak Juliet is discovered (to all outward appearances) dead in bed. The merriment is turned to wailing.

The end of the scene serves the same dramatic purpose as Scene iv (see pp. 99-100). It is a complete contrast in tone to the tragedy preceding it, and at the same time it links these tragic events with the everyday life of ordinary mortals—brings us "down to earth", so to speak. It is all in the day's work for the hired musicians whether they play for a wedding or a funeral, and they look on either dispassionately. A scene of (apparent) tragedy is sandwiched between two comic scenes, and this throws it up, making the tragedy seem more tragic against a touch of comedy and the comedy more comic against the tragedy. The audience knows that Juliet is not dead, of course, but the *effect* of her supposed death on the family is the same.

The tension is relieved, we feel glad to laugh after the strain of the first part of the scene.

fast, *i.e.* fast asleep.
she. *Cf.* note on "I", p. 92.
slug-a-bed, *lit.* slug in a bed, *i.e.* lazy creature.
your pennyworths, *i.e.* every bit of sleep you can.
set up his rest, determined, resolved.
Will it not be? *i.e.* will you not wake up?
down again! *i.e.* laid down again (after having dressed).
well-a-day. See note p. 87. *ALAS THE DAY.*
aqua-vitæ. See note p. 88. *BRANDY*
What noise is here? *i.e.* what is the meaning of the noise here?
heavy. *Cf.* note p. 87.
my only life, life itself to me.
For shame. Capulet is referring to the delay.
alack the day! See note on "well-a-day", p. 87.
out, Intensifies "alas!".

settled, congealed.

living, property. *Cf.* earning a living, or a clergyman's *living.*

to see, about seeing.

lasting, *i.e.* the long, unending.

poor. Capulet is thinking of her ill-timed death.

solace, find comfort.

Beguiled. See note p. 88.

Despised, *i.e.* by fate.

Uncomfortable, with no comfort.

solemnity. See note p. 66.

not, *i.e.* not now.

confusion, destruction. In the next line the word has more its modern sense.

his part in, *i.e.* his part in her.

promotion, *i.e.* by a marriage into the royal family. (Paris was the Prince's kinsman.)

heaven, *i.e.* idea of what was best.

well, *i.e.* in heaven.

rosemary. See note p. 9.

as the custom is. See note on "as the manner of our country is", p. 98.

reason's merriment, a laughing matter for reason.

festival. An adjective—festive. *Cf.* "funeral" in antithesis in the next line.

solemn. The context here clearly shows the Elizabethan meaning of the word. See note on "solemnity", p. 66 (also above).

them, themselves (reflexive). *Cf.* "her", note p. 94, and "Content thee", note p. 66.

ill, *i.e.* evil deed that you have done. This, by the way, is Old Testament, not Christian, teaching.

the case. The musician looks at his shabby instrument case.

'Heart's ease.' 'My heart is full of woe.' Both popular English songs at the end of the sixteenth century. The second is the chorus of a ballad called *A Pleasant New Ballad of Two Lovers,* by Richard Edwards. It is quoted later in the scene.

dump, sad song. *Cf.* "doleful dumps" later in the scene. Peter says that he wants a *"merry* dump" just for comic effect— cheap nonsensical humour which characters of low intelligence find funny.

soundly, thoroughly—as Old Mother Hubbard "Whipped them all *soundly* and sent them to bed". The pun on the word used to a musician is obvious.

the gleek. To "give the gleek" was to jeer.

give you the minstrel, call you (set you down as) a minstrel. (There may be an implied pun between "gleek" and "gleemen", another name for minstrels.) Minstrels were no longer held in good repute at the end of the sixteenth century. Minstrelsy became a dying craft after the invention of printing and minstrels were esteemed less and less as the years went on. In III. i Mercutio took offence because he thought (or affected to think) that Tybalt was calling them minstrels—"What, dost thou make us minstrels?".

give you the serving-creature, call you a servant. "Creature" adds a note of contempt. Notice that to call anyone a "minstrel" was as insulting as to call him a "serving-creature".

carry no crotchets, bear no insults. *Cf.* "crotchety".

re. fa. The second and fourth notes of the sol-fa scale (now usually spelt "ray" and "fah"). A pun on the word "note" follows.

put out. Again punning; (1) extinguish, (2) stick it out (to attack with it).

have at you. See note on "Have at thee", p. 52.

dry-beat. See note p. 84.

'When griping . . . sound.' See note on " 'Heart's ease.' 'My heart is full of woe' ", p. 102.

Catling. catgut.

Rebeck. A three-stringed fiddle.

for silver, *i.e.* to be paid.

Soundpost. The name of the piece of wood fixed near the bridge of a fiddle to keep the back and the belly apart.

cry you mercy, ask your pardon.

you are the singer. And therefore cannot "say". Peter is still playing with words.

sounding, *i.e.* the music they make.

'Then music . . . redress.' He completes the stanza he started above.

Jack. Not used as his name (which was Simon). See note p. 78.

REVISION QUESTIONS ON ACT IV

1. Describe the meeting of Juliet and Paris at Friar Laurence's cell (the only one in the play).

2. "I have a faint cold fear thrills through my veins." Describe the fears of Juliet just before she brought herself to swallow the potion.

3. In what frame of mind did Capulet prepare for the wedding feast? Prove your answer from the play.

4. Describe the way in which Juliet was discovered "dead" in bed on the morning which was to be the morning of her marriage with Paris.

5. Do you think that the deception practised on Juliet's family was justified?

6. What is the *dramatic* reason for the foolery of the musicians?

ACT V.   SCENE I   MANTUA A STREET

In Mantua Romeo's servant Balthasar brings him news of Juliet's death and burial, but no letters from Friar Laurence. Romeo buys some poison on the black market (in current idiom), intending to kill himself in Juliet's "monument" and so to be with her.

Notice the irony of a situation where bad news overwhelms Romeo just as he is rejoicing in his good spirits, expecting "joyful news". Compare how Capulet's heart was "wondrous light" the night before his daughter was found dead in the morning (end IV. ii). The feeling that ill-fortune is shadowing his love is strengthened, a foreboding present from the first (see pp. 15-16).

For comment on the description of the apothecary's shop, see p. 18.

flattering truth of sleep, *i.e.* dreams that flatter us they are true. The sense is that Romeo's dreams seem too good to be true.

My bosom's lord, *i.e.* love.

in, on.

I dreamt . . . dead. A reversal of the actual. Amongst all his happiness this gives a presentiment of evil without telling us just how things are going to happen.

an emperor, *i.e.* lord of all.

possess'd, enjoyed.

How now. Corresponding to our exclamation, "What now?". See note p. 59.

Dost . . . again. The way in which Romeo fires question after question at Balthasar without waiting for an answer is very natural: it shows the excitement of a lonely banished man on seeing someone with news. Notice that Romeo addresses his servant as "thou", but Balthasar his master as "you". The same convention is observed in Romeo's talk with the apothecary.

well. Balthasar is trying to break the news gently, using the word to mean (for himself) "in peace".

Capel. In Brooke's *Romeus and Juliet* Capel and Capulet are used indiscriminately.

presently. See note p. 97.

post, "post-horses", fresh horses kept at "posts" at regular intervals along a road: a traveller rode more quickly on relays of fresh horses. *Cf.* "post-haste". Notice that Balthasar comes in "booted".

office, duty. It was Balthasar's duty to bring news, whatever it was.

stars, *i.e.* my fate. See note on "star-cross'd", p. 50.

get . . . to-night. Notice the curt decisiveness of these commands.

import some misadventure, betoken some calamity. "Misadventure" was a stronger word then than now.

I will lie with thee to-night, *i.e.* as a corpse in a tomb.

means, *i.e.* means to do it.

I do remember an apothecary. Romeo has soon found his way about Mantua! See p. 10.

a'. See note p. 78.

noted, noticed.

weeds, clothes.

overwhelming brows, overhanging eyebrows, "beetle brows" (see note on "Here . . . me", p. 62).

of. The "of" is inserted because "culling" is a verbal noun.

simples, medicinal herbs.

meagre, thin, scraggy.

needy, *i.e.* bare (epithet transferred from the apothecary to his shop).

alligator stuff'd. The sign of an apothecary. In Shakespeare's day (when the man-in-the-street could not read) shopkeepers made known their trade by symbols; indeed, an Elizabethan street must have looked very picturesque. Some of these signs still survive, *e.g.* the barber's pole.

ill-shaped fishes, fish of evil shape.

beggarly account, very small number.

bladders, to hold liquids.

packthread, stout thread.

cakes of roses, dried rose petals crushed together for use as a perfume. Sachets of such were sold as late as the present century.

is present death, brings immediate death—to the apothecary by sentence of law (not to the purchaser by taking the poison). For "present" see note p. 97.

forerun, anticipate.

Hold. See note p. 97.

ducats. Silver or gold coins current in several European countries. In English money contemporary with the play a gold ducat was worth nearly ten shillings and a silver ducat about half as much, but the value varied greatly from state to state and from time to time. The point is that "forty ducats" was a goodly sum. They are spoken of in the singular ("is") because they are thought of as *one* sum of money, as is common (though not correct) in dealings with English coinage to-day.

soon-speeding gear, quickly-working stuff.

fatal, *i.e.* death-dealing.

he, person.

utters. *Cf.* the *uttering* of false coins.

bare, *i.e.* half-starved.

Need . . . eyes, it can be seen from your eyes that want and oppression are killing you. For "starveth" see note on "starved", p. 55.

Contempt, *i.e.* the cause of other men's contempt.

hangs upon thy back, *i.e.* in your "tatter'd weeds". Notice the singular verbs with plural subjects in "starveth" and "hangs": this is common in Shakespearean English where the two subjects are combined in one idea. See also note on "ducats", above.

not . . . nor. See note on "Nor no", p. 61. The sense of the second half of the line is, "Neither is the world's law thy friend".

affords, provides.

I sell . . . none, *i.e.* gold is a worse poison than this drug. (It has been proved so in this transaction.)

in flesh, *i.e.* better covered with flesh.

cordial and not poison. Because it will be the means of sending him to be with Juliet.

Friar Laurence's Cell.

ACT V.   SCENE II

Friar Laurence's messenger to Romeo returns to his cell, having been unable to deliver his letter.

Friar Laurence is anxious, and sends him to fetch a crowbar, for now he must go alone to the Capulet "monument" ready for when Juliet awakes.

Franciscan. See note on "Saint Francis", p. 74.

bare-foot, *i.e.* Franciscan. The Franciscans were enjoined to walk barefoot, and friars usually travelled in pairs.

associate, accompany.

Seal'd up, *i.e.* put the official seal on, indicating that no one was allowed to enter or leave the house. This was the sixteenth-century method of isolating people with the plague (see p. 18).

stay'd, delayed.

they, *i.e.* the messengers.

nice. See note p. 85.

charge, importance, weight.

dear, great. See note on "dear account", p. 67.

crow, crowbar.

accidents, events.

living corse. Oxymoron. See note on "loving hate", p. 54. For "corse" see note p. 88.

ACT V.   SCENE III

The churchyard.

Accompanied by his page Paris brings flowers to lay on Juliet's tomb. A moment or two later Romeo, likewise accompanied by his man, comes to the tomb with tools to open it. Both send off their servants to stand "aloof". As Romeo opens the tomb Paris challenges him. Romeo speaks him fair (not knowing who he is), but Paris will not desist: they fight, Romeo slays his opponent, and it is with regret that he sees that it is Paris. He kisses Juliet and takes his poison.

From the other end of the churchyard comes Friar Laurence, just in time to see Juliet awake. But it is too late. Finding Romeo dead she stabs herself with his dagger.

Meanwhile Paris's page has called the "watch". They arrest the Friar and Romeo's servant until the Prince comes. Then the Friar tells what has happened, and the Prince points the moral that the hatred of Capulet and Montague has brought its own punishment, and at sunrise on a gloomy morning the two life-long enemies shake hands and at long last bury their ancient quarrel.

thy. Notice how Paris and Romeo both address their servants as "thou" ("thy"), but Balthasar's reply addresses Romeo as "you". Similarly, Paris and Romeo, enemies, address each other as "thou".

aloof, apart.

Yet, further—an order amending his first.

yond. See note p. 67.

yew-trees. Traditionally associated with churchyards.

thee. Reflexive. *Cf.* note on "Content thee", p. 66.

all along, *i.e.* flat on the ground.

But. See note p. 71.

stand, *i.e.* be, remain. He does not mean "even to stand, let alone lie down": the word "stand" has no reference to Paris's command to "lay thee all along".

sweet water, *i.e.* perfumed water. Perhaps holy water. This speech of Paris is set in the form of a sestet of a (Shakespearean) sonnet (see note on "PROLOGUE", p. 50). This gives it more the effect of a set ritual—"true love's rite".

wanting. See note on "wanting of", p. 71.

keep, observe.

cross, thwart.

mattock. Like a pickaxe, only with an arched blade at one side.

all. See note p. 99.

Why, *i.e.* the reason why.

chiefly . . . employment. This is just to allay any suspicion Balthasar might have. "Dear" = important: *cf.* note p. 106.

jealous, suspicious.

The time. Romeo probably means the time after Juliet's death, but perhaps simply the dead of night.

empty. And therefore savage.

that. A money present.

For all this same, notwithstanding all this.

His locks I fear. Not on his own account, of course, but Balthasar fears what Romeo may do to himself.

despite, defiance.

with, *i.e.* owing to.

Stop . . . Montague! This is the only time in the play that Romeo and Paris meet on the stage—though both attended the Capulet ball (I. v).

Can vengeance . . . death? Paris thinks that Romeo has come to desecrate the Capulet tomb, in particular the body of Tybalt.

gone, *i.e.* dead in the tomb.

affright thee. The implication is, "And prevent your hindering me".

another sin, *i.e.* killing you.

defy thy conjurations, reject thy solemn appeals.

have at thee. See note p. 52.

watch. The Elizabethan police.

peruse, look closely at.

Mercutio's kinsman. Both Mercutio and Paris were kinsmen of the Prince.

betossed, storm-tossed.

attend him, pay attention to what he was saying.

triumphant, splendid.

lantern, *i.e.* lit by the light of Juliet's beauty.

feasting presence, festal presence-chamber (of a monarch).

Death. Abstract for concrete, as often in Shakespeare.

a dead man. A vivid reference to his own impending death.

keepers, attendants. Romeo is not necessarily thinking of men at the point of death in prison.

A lightning before death. A proverbial phrase to describe the not uncommon burst of vigour just before death, a vigour in spirits as well as in body, as if nature is making a last effort.

honey, *i.e.* sweetness. (Honey was the regular sweetening substance in Old England.)

sheet, winding-sheet.

cousin. Romeo is undoubtedly using the word for the actual relationship—Tybalt would be his cousin (by marriage to Juliet). See note p. 54.

shake the yoke. The metaphor is the entirely appropriate one of a beast of burden coming home at the end of the day and shaking off his yoke.

stars. See note p. 104.

dateless, *i.e.* eternal.

engrossing, swallowing everything up, gathering everything in.

conduct, conductor. See note p. 84. Romeo is addressing the vial of poison.

true apothecary. Romeo can feel the poison overcoming him at once: he acknowledges that the apothecary has not played him false.

Saint Francis. See note p. 74.

stumbled. A sign of ill-omen. This superstition goes back a long way—there is the classical example of William the Conqueror's stumbling when he first set foot on English soil and his men interpreting it as a bad sign.

I dreamt. Does Balthasar really believe it to be a dream or does he put it like this to avoid admitting that he had defied his master's orders?

masterless, *i.e.* lying on the floor, not in the possession of their owners (masters).

discolour'd, *i.e.* by blood.

unkind, unnatural.

comfortable, bringing strength and comfort. *Cf.* "Uncomfort-able", note p. 102. Both words were stronger in meaning in Shakespeare's time.

timeless, untimely, with perhaps a play on the meaning "eternal".

churl. This, of course, is said in a kindly way.

restorative. In normal circumstances Romeo's kiss would be a restorative.

attach, arrest.

this. Singular because the "two days" are thought of as a single span of time. *Cf.* note on "ducats", p. 105.

ground of, reason for.

circumstance. See note p. 80.

stay, *i.e.* keep in custody. More forceful than on p. 106.

our. See note on "our further pleasure", p. 53.

With open outcry. A metaphor from hunting, when the dogs are "in full cry" after the game.

startles in, alarms, shocks.

know. See note p. 91.

mista'en, *i.e.* mistaken its proper house.

his house, *i.e.* its sheath. *Cf.* note on "his native progress, but surcease", p. 97.

warns, *i.e.* summons.

my old age. See pp. 34-35.

untaught, ill-bred. Again said kindly, like Juliet's "churl".

is. The idea of "manners"—good breeding—is a singular one. *Cf.* note on "hangs upon thy back", p. 105.

to press . . . grave? As if he were pushing through a doorway in front of his father.

the mouth of outrage, your outbursts of feeling.

ambiguities, things which are not clear.

spring. head. descent. Metaphors from a stream flowing down from its source, standing for the beginning and the sequence of "these ambiguities".

general . . . death, *i.e.* at the head of your woes (to get venge-ance or at least inflict punishment) even if it leads to the death of those responsible.

mischance be slave to patience, *i.e.* disaster be ruled by patience.

the parties of suspicion, those on whom suspicion falls.

the greatest, *i.e.* the greatest "party of suspicion".

able to do least, *i.e.* physically.

Doth make, do inform, witness. Here again two subjects in close association have a singular verb.

of this direful murder. This adjectival phrase relates to "time and place".

both . . . excused, *i.e.* to impeach myself condemned and to purge (clear, defend) myself excused. The friar acknowledges that he can be accused of being the cause of these deaths (his con-demnation), but not that it was his intention (that is his excuse).

in, of, about.

date of breath, time I have to live.

their stol'n marriage-day, the day of their stolen (secret, steal-thy) marriage.

siege. The metaphor suggests that she was surrounded by grief and could not escape from it.

mean, means.

form, *i.e.* appearance.

as. A redundant word used in expressions of time, retained now only in the phrases "as yet", "as from".

stay'd. See note p. 106.

closely, secretly.

She wakes. Notice this dramatic transition to the present tense, making the effect more crisp and forceful. The effect is similar (but in reverse order of time) to that of l. 87, where Romeo calls himself "a dead man".

this work of heaven, *i.e.* Romeo's death.

We still . . . man. Practically the same words as Juliet used of the friar (IV. iii. 29).

in post, in a great hurry, post-haste. See note p. 104.

going, as he went.

raised, sent for, called, summoned.

made your master, was your master doing.

make good, confirm.

therewithal, with that

scourge, *i.e.* punishment.

your joys, *i.e.* Juliet and Romeo respectively.

winking at, closing my eyes to.

a brace of kinsmen, *i.e.* Mercutio and Paris.

jointure. A wife's marriage-settlement from her husband (or his family): the opposite of a dowry, which was the portion given by *her own* family. Capulet says that Montague's handshake (friendship) is all that he can ask from him for his daughter's jointure.

rate, value.

rich, valuable.

sacrifices of our enmity, offerings of our hatred (which has now ceased).

glooming, gloomy. The play ends with the sestet of a Shakespearean sonnet. See note on "PROLOGUE", p. 50.

REVISION QUESTIONS ON ACT V

1. Describe the apothecary's shop.

2. Did Romeo find it easy to obtain poison from him? Make a few observations confirming your answer.

3. What was the "unhappy fortune" which prevented Romeo from getting the Friar's letter?

4. Describe the meeting of Romeo and Paris (the only one in the play.)

5. Is the Friar's account of events to the Prince substantially correct? Give an outline of his speech.

QUESTIONS

GENERAL QUESTIONS

1. Describe the chapter of accidents which led to the deaths of Romeo and Juliet.

2. Mention any discrepancies of time in the play.

3. Make a list of all the characters in the play who come to a fatal end.

4. Where did Shakespeare draw the material for *Romeo and Juliet*? Point out and comment on any additions or alterations made by him.

5. Comment on the structure of *Romeo and Juliet*.

6. What is the importance of the family feud in the play?

7. "Although swift when its time is analysed the play is not so swift in its general impression" (p. 9). What developments do you notice in the characters of Romeo and Juliet between the first and the last Act?

8. "O! I am Fortune's fool." Do you consider this a fair assessment of the situation?

9. Do you agree with the Friar that Romeo's death is a "work of heaven"?

10. In the Prologue Romeo and Juliet are described as "star-cross'd lovers" and reference is made to their "death-mark'd love". They themselves speak like this. Do you think that Shakespeare wants to create the impression that their death is brought about by a cruel overwhelming Fate, by sheer accident or by their own wilfulness, or by some or all of these?

11. Comment on Juliet's resource, courage and depth of feeling, and say whether you consider these beyond a girl of fourteen.

12. "My dismal scene I needs must act alone." What is the dramatic value of the lack of sympathy between Juliet and the other people of the Capulet household?

13. In *Romeo and Juliet* hero and heroine come to an untimely end. Can you account, therefore, for the fact that the play gives you entertainment?

14. The love-scenes are beautiful as poetry, but how far are they dramatically important?

15. Write a character-sketch of Mercutio, basing your answer upon (*a*) what other people say about him, (*b*) what he says about himself.

16. Describe the characters of Mercutio and the Nurse, showing how they provide comedy and relief.

17. What is the difference between the chatter of Mercutio and that of the Nurse?

18. Can the character of Capulet in Act III be reconciled with his character in Act I?

19. The title-page of Brooke's poem refers to the "Subtill Counsels and Practises of an old Fryer". Do you think the Friar of the play a wise man or a fool, an honest man or an underhand schemer?

20. Write a paragraph on the character of Benvolio and one on the character of Tybalt.

21. Give the substance of any two soliloquies (by different people) and in each case say what they show of the character of the speaker.

22. Mention three situations of intense emotion in this play and describe one of them.

23. Point out two striking character-contrasts in *Romeo and Juliet* and in each case work out the contrast fully.

24. Name three comic characters in *Romeo and Juliet*, say what you think of them as comic characters (comparing and contrasting them) and say to what extent they make the tragedy better or worse.

25. Would anything be lost (or gained) if Rosaline were never mentioned?

26. Does the reconciliation between the Capulets and the Montagues make a good ending to the play, or is it an anti-climax in which no one is interested?

27. To what period of Shakespeare's artistic development would you assign this play? Give your reasons.

28. Show from *Romeo and Juliet* how Shakespeare varies his poetic effects to suit different dramatic situations.

29. Mention any passages which give a sense of foreboding for the future.

30. Quote or refer to any superbly beautiful passages of poetry in the play, pointing out in what their beauty consists.

31. Act II has been called the most poetic in the play. Do you think the tribute deserved? Say why, with close reference to the text.

32. Quote or refer to any passages of poetry that have a loathsome fascination, and say how the effect is produced.

33. Choose (*a*) five examples of Shakespeare's imagery which appeal to you, and (*b*) three examples of (i) simile, (ii) metaphor, with comments.

34. In *Romeo and Juliet* the audience is given information which is denied to some of the characters. Give some examples and show the variety of effects Shakespeare achieved by this device.

35. Does the punning increase your enjoyment of the play or do you think that it is overdone? Which persons of the play indulge in it most?

36. Describe two or three considerable passages in prose, and one in rhyming verse, and account for the medium in each case.

37. Give three reasons which, in your opinion, account for the popularity of *Romeo and Juliet* on the stage.

38. Which part in the play would you most like to act? Which do you think is the most difficult part to act? In each case give your reasons.

39. What features of *Romeo and Juliet* may be ascribed to Elizabethan stage conditions?

40. By what means has the text of Shakespeare's plays been determined?

CONTEXT QUESTIONS

Answer the questions upon the following passages.

1.   O, she doth teach the torches to burn bright!
    It seems she hangs upon the cheek of night
    Like a rich jewel in an Ethiop's ear;
    Beauty too rich for use, for earth too dear!
    So shows a snowy dove trooping with crows,
    As yonder lady o'er her fellows shows.
    The measure done, I'll watch her place of stand,
    And, touching hers, make blessed my rude hand.
    Did my heart love till now? forswear it, sight!
    For I ne'er saw true beauty till this night.

(a) Where was "yonder lady"? Describe the occasion.

(b) Why had Romeo gone to this place?

(c) Romeo's friends had a purpose in persuading him to go. Was it successful?

(d) What was it about Juliet that touched off Romeo's love?

(e) Give the meaning of "Beauty too rich for use".

(f) Someone for whom it was not intended heard this speech, or at least Romeo's voice. With what results?

(g) What is the predominant contrast in the two similes?

(h) Is there any particular reason why the speech is in rhyme?

2.   Hark, how they knock! Who's there? Romeo,
      arise;
    Thou wilt be taken. Stay awhile! Stand up;
                         [*Knocking.*
    Run to my study. By and by! God's will,
    What simpleness is this! I come, I come!
                         [*Knocking.*
    Who knocks so hard? whence come you? what's
      your will?

(a) What is the dramatic effect of this knocking?

(b) How does the style show the agitation of the speaker?

(c) Write out the speech, separating the parts spoken to different people.

(d) What is the meaning of "simpleness"?

(e) Who was it knocking?

(f) What did the caller come for?

3. O, she is lame! love's heralds should be thoughts,
   Which ten times faster glide than the sun's beams,
   Driving back shadows over louring hills:
   Therefore do nimble-pinion'd doves draw love,
   And therefore hath the wind-swift Cupid wings.
   Now is the sun upon the highmost hill
   Of this day's journey, and from nine till twelve
   Is three long hours, yet she is not come.
   Had she affections and warm youthful blood,
   She would be as swift in motion as a ball;
   My words would bandy her to my sweet love,
   And his to me:
   But old folks, many feign as they were dead;
   Unwieldy, slow, heavy and pale as lead.

(a) "Yet she is not come." Who is awaited?

(b) With what particular message?

(c) When the "herald" came, how was the message given?

(d) Explain the references to classical mythology in lines 4-5.

(e) What is the meaning of "affections", "feign"?

(f) Whereabouts in the scene does this passage come? What is its dramatic effect?

(g) There is in this passage one of the predominant contrasts of the play. What is it?

(h) Why do you think that the last couplet is in rhyme?

(i) Is there any purpose, do you think, in the short line near the end?

4. If I may trust the flattering truth of sleep,
   My dreams presage some joyful news at hand:
   My bosom's lord sits lightly in his throne,
   And all this day an unaccustom'd spirit
   Lifts me above the ground with cheerful thoughts.
   I dreamt my lady came and found me dead—
   Strange dream, that gives a dead man leave to think!—
   And breathed such life with kisses in my lips,
   That I revived and was an emperor.
   Ah me! how sweet is love itself possess'd,
   When but love's shadows are so rich in joy!

(*a*) Say in your own words why the speaker is cheerful.

(*b*) What is the dramatic effect of his exhilaration *just at this moment?*

(*c*) What is the news that follows post-haste?

(*d*) What is the dramatic effect of lines 6 and 8 in view of subsequent events?

(*e*) Mention another occasion in the play when someone feels very happy just before calamity.

5.   Why, is not this better now than groaning for love?
      now art thou sociable, now art thou Romeo; now art
      thou what thou art, by art as well as by nature: for
      this drivelling love is like a great natural, that runs
      lolling up and down to hide his bauble.

(*a*) What has brought about the change in Romeo?

(*b*) Is the speaker aware of it?

(*c*) Explain (i) the pun, (ii) the meaning of the simile.

(*d*) Why is this speech very important in one's consideration of Romeo's character?

(*e*) Why do you think that it is in prose?

6.   Beautiful tyrant! fiend angelical!
      Dove-feather'd raven! wolvish-ravening lamb!
      Despised substance of divinest show!
      Just opposite to what thou justly seem'st,
      A damned saint, an honourable villain!

(*a*) What figure of speech is this called? What other character used it in similar quick succession, and on what occasion?

(*b*) Explain the pun on ''just'' and ''justly''. Is it true to life that the speaker should jest at this moment?

(*c*) What calamity has just overtaken the speaker?

7.   It is the lark that sings so out of tune,
      Straining harsh discords and unpleasing sharps.
      Some say the lark makes sweet division;
      This doth not so, for she divideth us:
      Some say the lark and loathed toad change eyes;
      O, now I would they had changed voices too!

(*a*) What is the significance of the lark's song on the present occasion?

(*b*) Why does the lark seem to sing "out of tune" on this particular morning?

(*c*) Why is it wished that the lark and the toad had changed voices?

(*d*) Explain the musical terms in the passage.

8.   O, here
Will I set up my everlasting rest,
And shake the yoke of inauspicious stars
From this world-wearied flesh. Eyes, look your last!
Arms, take your last embrace! and, lips, O you
The doors of breath, seal with a righteous kiss
A dateless bargain to engrossing death!
Come, bitter conduct, come, unsavoury guide!

(*a*) "Here." Where?

(*b*) Where else does the speaker refer to the unequal odds of a life battling against a fate writ in the stars?

(*c*) "This world-wearied flesh." Have you any comments to make on this phrase, either regarding the character of the speaker or the whole effect of the play?

(*d*) Who is the "unsavoury guide"?

(*e*) Give a free rendering of the passage in your own words.

9.   Heaven and yourself
Had part in this fair maid; now heaven hath all,
And all the better is it for the maid:
Your part in her you could not keep from death;
But heaven keeps his part in eternal life.
The most you sought was her promotion,
For 'twas your heaven she should be advanced:
And weep ye now, seeing she is advanced
Above the clouds, as high as heaven itself?
O, in this love, you love your child so ill,
That you run mad, seeing that she is well:
She 's not well married that lives married long,
But she 's best married that dies married young.
Dry up your tears, and stick your rosemary
On this fair corse, and, as the custom is,
In all her best array bear her to church:
For though fond nature bids us all lament,
Yet nature's tears are reason's merriment.

(*a*) Would you call this "cold comfort"?

(*b*) What information could the speaker have given that would *really* have given comfort?

(*c*) Would you call the speech callous or deceitful, or do you regard it as justified by the circumstances?

(*d*) "Advanced"—in what way?

(*e*) "As the custom is." Where was this the custom? There is a custom of Shakespeare's England referred to: what is it?

(*f*) Give the meaning of the last line in your own words.

(*g*) In what way does the verse emphasise the conventional nature of this consolation?

(*h*) What is the reason for the rhyming couplet at the end?

10. Therefore, out of thy long-experienced time,
     Give me some present counsel; or, behold,
     'Twixt my extremes and me this bloody knife
     Shall play the umpire, arbitrating that
     Which the commission of thy years and art
     Could to no issue of true honour bring.
     Be not so long to speak; I long to die,
     If what thou speak'st speak not of remedy.

(*a*) Give the meaning of the passage as closely as you can in your own words.

(*b*) Upon what problem was "present counsel" sought?

(*c*) Why did the problem seem particularly urgent at that time?

(*d*) Romeo and Juliet are both prone to thoughts of suicide when frustrated. What effect does this have upon the credibility of the last scene?

11. A torch for me; let wantons light of heart
     Tickle the senseless rushes with their heels,
     For I am proverb'd with a grandsire phrase;
     I'll be a candle-holder, and look on.
     The game was ne'er so fair, and I am done.

(*a*) Why did he want to be a "candle-holder"?

(*b*) What sort of picture of a dance in Old England do the words "rushes" and "candle-holder" give you?

(*c*) What contrast implicit in the play is emphasised here?

(*d*) Explain the last line in detail.

12. Then have at you with my wit! I will dry-beat you
    with an iron wit, and put up my iron dagger. Answer
    me like men:

    > 'When griping grief the heart doth wound
    > And doleful dumps the mind oppress,
    > Then music with her silver sound'—

    why 'silver sound'? why 'music with her silver
    sound'?

    (a) Express the first two sentences in your own words.

    (b) What answers were given to the question? By whom
    (names are not necessary) and on what occasion?

    (c) What are the dramatic purposes of a bit of fun at this
    particular stage?

    (d) Why is the speech (saving for the song) in prose?

    (e) What class of song is it?

13. The grey-ey'd morn smiles on the frowning night,
    Chequering the eastern clouds with streaks of light,
    And flecked darkness like a drunkard reels
    From forth day's path and Titan's fiery wheels:
    Now, ere the sun advance his burning eye,
    The day to cheer and night's dank dew to dry,
    I must up-fill this osier cage of ours
    With baleful weeds and precious-juicéd flowers.

    (a) What has the gathering of weeds and flowers to do with
    the play?

    (b) Who was Titan?

    (c) Give the meaning of the last four lines in your own words.

    (d) Several passages in *Romeo and Juliet* describe the early
    morning. Mention one other.

14. I have an interest in your hate's proceeding,
    My blood for your rude brawls doth lie a-bleeding;
    But I'll amerce you with so strong a fine
    That you shall all repent the loss of mine.
    I will be deaf to pleading and excuses;
    Nor tears nor prayers shall purchase out abuses:
    Therefore use none; let Romeo hence in haste,
    Else, when he's found, that hour is his last.
    Bear hence this body and attend our will:
    Mercy but murders, pardoning those that kill.

(a) At what particular point in the affairs of Romeo and Juliet was this speech uttered?

(b) Explain the import of the first two lines.

(c) Give the meaning of the passage as closely as you can in your own words.

(d) "Let Romeo hence in haste." Where did he go to?

(e) "This body." Whose body? Comment on this line in relation to Elizabethan stage conditions.

(f) Do you think that the speaker was right in (i) letting his personal feelings influence his judgment, (ii) being "deaf to pleading and excuses"?

15. Going to find a bare-foot brother out,
     One of our order, to associate me,
     Here in this city visiting the sick,
     And finding him, the searchers of the town,
     Suspecting that we both were in a house
     Where the infectious pestilence did reign,
     Seal'd up the doors and would not let us forth.

(a) To what order did a "bare-foot brother" belong?

(b) Comment on the last line in the light of regulations in Old England.

(c) What is the effect of this occurrence upon the events of the play?

(d) What was the next task that the speaker was given to do?

16.   What should she do here?
     My dismal scene I needs must act alone.
     Come, vial.
     What if this mixture do not work at all?
     Shall I be married then to-morrow morning?
     No, no: this shall forbid it. Lie thou there.

(a) In what tone of voice do you think that the first line should be said? Why?

(b) What is the effect of the second line upon the feelings of the audience?

(c) How would you account for the shortness of the third line?

(d) Did the mixture "work" according to plan?

(e) "Lie thou there." What does she lay down to make doubly sure? On what other occasion did she display one of these?

(f) What is the effect of the short sentences?

17. Now, afore God, I am so vexed, that every part
   about me quivers. Scurvy knave! Pray you, sir,
   a word: and as I told you, my young lady bade me
   inquire you out; what she bade me say I will keep
   to myself: but first let me tell ye, if ye should lead
   her into a fool's paradise, as they say, it were a very
   gross kind of behaviour, as they say.

(a) Why was she "vexed"?

(b) "Scurvy knave!" Whom is she denouncing?

(c) Little would be lost if she did "keep to herself" what her lady bade her say. Why?

(d) What can be seen of her character from this short extract?

18. Hist! Romeo, hist! O, for a falconer's voice,
   To lure this tassel-gentle back again!
   Bondage is hoarse, and may not speak aloud,
   Else would I tear the cave where Echo lies,
   And make her airy tongue more hoarse than mine,
   With repetition of my Romeo's name.

(a) Did she succeed in luring the "tassel-gentle" back again?

(b) What is the meaning of "Bondage is hoarse"?

(c) Who was Echo?

(d) Where was Juliet speaking from?

(e) Mention any other English sport besides falconry referred to in the play.

19. Marry, sir, 'tis an ill cook that cannot lick his own
   fingers: therefore he that cannot lick his fingers goes
   not with me.

(a) Why were cooks needed just then? How many?

(b) What is the force of "Marry", and the sense of "Goes not with me"?

(c) How were these facetious remarks received?

(d) Why are they in prose?

(e) Part of the purpose of this episode is to fill in a time lapse. What happens elsewhere meanwhile?

20. Sir Paris, I will make a desperate tender
Of my child's love: I think she will be ruled
In all respects by me; nay, more, I doubt it not.
Wife, go you to her ere you go to bed;
Acquaint her here of my son Paris' love;
And bid her, mark you me, on Wednesday next—
But, soft! what day is this?

(*a*) What do you understand by "a desperate tender"?

(*b*) "I think she will be ruled in all respects by me." What is the name in dramatic criticism given to such a statement?

(*c*) "Wife, go you to her ere you go to bed." Why does this direction give a thrill of suspense to the audience? Outline what took place when his wife took the message.

(*d*) Why does he call Paris his "son"?

(*e*) "Wednesday." Was this day fixed and kept?

(*f*) What is the force of "Soft!"?

(*g*) "What day is this?" What is the answer? What time of day was it?

KEY TO CONTEXT QUESTIONS

(Where no line is given, it is owing to variation of numbering in different editions.)

(1) I. v. *Romeo*, (2) III. iii. 74-78, (3) II. v. 4-17, (4) V. i. 1-11, (5) II. iv. *Mercutio*, (6) III. ii. *Juliet*, (7) III. v. 27-32, (8) V. iii. 109-116, (9) IV. v. *Friar*, (10) IV. i. 60-67, (11) I. iv. 35-39, (12) IV. v. *Peter*, (13) II. iii. 1-8, (14) III. i. *Prince*, (15) V. ii. 4-11, (16) IV. iii. 18-23, (17) II. iv. *Nurse*, (18) II. ii. 159-164, (19) IV. ii. 6-8, (20) III. iv. 12-18.

PASSAGES SUGGESTED FOR MEMORISING

I. iv. 55, any part of Mercutio's "Queen Mab" speech; 107, Romeo's last speech: v. 48, Romeo's speech beginning, "O, she doth teach the torches to burn bright!" There is much worth learning in II. ii (see pp. 41 and 70): any part of the Friar's first speech in iii: vi. 24-29. III. v. 1-16, 26-35, 54-57. IV. iii. 14-23 and a few more lines of this speech, including 55-58. V. i. 1-11, 40-48: iii. 109-120.

PRINTED AT THE BURLINGTON PRESS, FOXTON, NEAR CAMBRIDGE, ENGLAND